Palgrave Studies in African and Development Economics

Series Editor
Arkebe Oqubay
British Academy Global Professor
SOAS University of London
London, UK

This series provides a wide-ranging analysis of African economics, development economics, and global transformation. Combing theoretical and empirical evidence, it offers thoughtful and policy relevant insight to the economic challenges and opportunities seen within the developing world. It engages with emerging and topical debates, including issues relating to sustainable development, food security, and the green transition, to make sure countries in Africa and the developing world are included in these important discussions.

Stephen Chan

The Economic Transformation and Political Economy of Zambia

The Search for Modernity, Equity and Principle

palgrave
macmillan

Stephen Chan
SOAS University of London
London, UK

With Contributions by
Hangwei Li
Bonn, Germany

McDonald Chipenzi
Lusaka, Zambia

Cynthia M. Kamwengo
Newnham College
University of Cambridge
Cambridge, UK

ISSN 3004-9601 ISSN 3004-961X (electronic)
Palgrave Studies in African and Development Economics
ISBN 978-3-031-93029-4 ISBN 978-3-031-93030-0 (eBook)
https://doi.org/10.1007/978-3-031-93030-0

This Palgrave Macmillan imprint is published by the registered company Springer Nature Switzerland AG.
The registered company address is: Gewerbestrasse 11, 6330 Cham, Switzerland

Competing Interests

The author has no competing interests to declare that are relevant to the content of this manuscript.

Contents

Notes on Contributors

Stephen Chan is Professor of World Politics at SOAS University of London, where he was also Foundation Dean of Law and Social Sciences. He has received state honours from both the United Kingdom and Zambia. He won the 2010 International Studies Association accolade, *Eminent Scholar in International Development*, and has been Konrad Adenauer Chair of Academic Excellence at Bir Zeit University in Palestine, and George Soros Chair of Public Policy at the Central European University.

McDonald Chipenzi has served as a Commissioner at the Electoral Commission of Zambia (ECZ), Executive Director of the Governance, Elections, Advocacy, Research Services (GEARS) Initiative, and Vice and Chairperson of the Council of Non-Governmental Organisations (CNGOs) in Zambia, Research and Information Officer and later as Executive Director—Foundation for Democratic Process (FODEP).

Cynthia M. Kamwengo is a research fellow at the Margaret Anstee Centre for Global Studies, Newnham College, University of Cambridge.

Hangwei Li is a senior researcher at the German Institute of Development and Sustainability, having also held appointments in China and at Harvard. She has also won a United Nations prize for her journalism and has travelled widely in Africa.

CHAPTER 1

Introduction: Building New Worlds Reaching for the Stars

Abstract As Zambia entered independence, despite the modest legacy of higher education from the colonial era, the imagination was one of modernity. Despite lampooning from the metropolitan West, even going into space was imagined. But the country faced schism even before it was born. Independence was a race both for modernity and against rebellion.

Keywords Astronaut • Rebel church • Robin Hood • Mine ownership • Lozi kingship

Writing in *The New Yorker* in 2017, Namwali Serpell seemed to hover between the suggestions that the 'Zambia Space Program' of 1964 was a subtle satire of the superpowers' space race—it proclaimed that Zambia would beat both the USA and the Soviet Union to the moon (and do so in a space craft piloted by a very attractive teenage girl)—and that it was a 'cover' of sorts for an activist, a protective device for someone who had campaigned against the British for Zambian independence.[1]

Time magazine's coverage of the 24 October 1964 independence celebrations—in which the new Zambian President, Kenneth Kaunda, had

[1] Namwali Serpell, 'The Zambian "Afronaut" who wanted to join the Space Race', *The New Yorker*, 11 March 2017.

S. Chan, *The Economic Transformation and Political Economy of Zambia*, Palgrave Studies in African and Development Economics, https://doi.org/10.1007/978-3-031-93030-0_1

preached the need for national and international harmony—added its own whimsical end note:

> One noted Zambian failed to share in all the harmony. He is Edward Mukuka Nkoloso, a grade-school science teacher and the director of Zambia's National Academy of Science, Space Research and Philosophy, who claimed the goings-on interfered with his space program to beat the U.S. and the Soviet Union to the moon. Already Nkoloso is training twelve Zambian astronauts, including a curvaceous 16-year-old girl, by spinning them around a tree in an oil drum and teaching them to walk on their hands, "the only way humans can walk on the moon."[2]

Some of Nkoloso's training methods were indeed novel—although each referred itself in some way to NASA practice. Thus, the rolling of his Afronauts downhill while encased in an oil drum was meant to simulate g-forces. The swinging from a rope tied to a high tree (with the rope suddenly cut at the highest point of the swing) was meant to simulate free-fall. And he himself wryly noted—as Serpell recounts—that people would laugh on the other side of their faces when he planted a Zambian flag on the moon.

The make-shift technology of the training sparked many wry comments. Some of the more ribald were accused of poking fun at uneducated Africans. The suggestions of deliberate satire or political cover came later. There is a third reading: Nkoloso was a person of great imagination to be sure, but he was a person very much of the twentieth century, and he shared the drive and longing for modernity, which then shaped so much of the aspiration of what was called the 'developing world'. If seek development, why not go for the max? Why not, after all, a space programme? Nkoloso was born in 1919 and fought in World War II. He became a Sergeant and was awarded the Soviet Jubilee Medal 'Forty Years of Victory in the Great Patriotic War 1941–1945', awarded retrospectively after its coinage in 1985. He did indeed participate in agitation for independence from Britain. Later, he achieved a law degree from the University of Zambia. He was certain Mars was inhabited but forbade his astronauts, after landing, from seeking to convert the Martians to Christianity. His space craft, D-Kalu 1, was made from aluminium and Zambian copper—and was named in honour of Kenneth Kaunda. As a multispecies-ist,

[2] Quoted, Serpell, ibid.

Nkoloso envisaged that his 17-year-old astronaut, Matha Mwambwa, would share the credit for reaching Mars with two cats. He applied to UNESCO for £7 million and to other unspecified sources for $1.9 billion. He was nothing short of ambition and self-belief—but the country of 1964 required every ounce of self-belief.

Although Kenneth Kaunda's own account of the independence struggle, *Zambia Shall be Free*,[3] was prefaced by a glowing Foreword by Sir Stewart Gore-Brown, an atypical legislative figure in Northern Rhodesia who believed in African political equality, Gore-Brown was by no means a representative of all white settler opinion.[4] Gore-Brown pithily suggests that Kaunda's book, published two years before Northern Rhodesia's independence as Zambia, 'represents the feelings of the great majority of sensible people, European as well as African', but this suggests that minority feeling still existed, not sensible and sceptical. We shall return to certain European attitudes in the mining sector, but the African attitudes were also far from unanimous in terms of Kaunda's own leadership. Harry Nkumbula, also befriended by Gore-Brown, was, like Kaunda, a campaigning activist for independence.[5] He was President of the African National Congress founded in 1951—with Kaunda as Secretary-General. They were not initially successful in calls for strike action, particularly in the mining sector, and the two men were imprisoned for two months in 1955 for distributing 'subversive literature'. Kaunda split from Nkumbula in 1958, ostensibly because of the latter's authoritarianism, and went back to prison for nine months for his activities and, upon his release in 1959, was made President of the United National Independence Party (UNIP) formed during the time of his incarceration. Nkumbula entered various alliances with Kaunda before independence but became leader of the opposition afterwards. In 1973, just after Zambia had become a one-party state, he had to join UNIP but, together with Simon Kapwepwe, opposed Kaunda for the party leadership in 1978. They were ruthlessly outmanoeuvred by Kaunda, but the bitterness of the rivalry became a part of

[3] London: Heinemann, 1962.

[4] Christina Lamb, *The Africa House: The Story of an English Gentleman and his African Dream*, London: Harper Collins, 2005.

[5] Hugh Macmillan, 'Nkumbula, Harry Mwaanga', *Oxford Dictionary of National Biography*, Oxford: Oxford University Press, 2004. Giacomo Macola, *Liberal Nationalism in Central Africa: A Biography of Harry Mwaanga Nkumbula*, N.Y.: Palgrave Macmillan, 2010. Goodwin B. Mwangilwa, *Harry Nkumbula: A Biography*, Lusaka: Multimedia, 1982. 'Harry Nkumbula dies; led African Congress', *New York Times*, 10 October 1983.

Zambian political history, especially the rivalry between Kaunda and Kapwepwe—who had been Kaunda's Vice President from 1967 to 1970.[6]

All this is to say that the saintly and almost sanctimonious image of Kaunda that has sometimes been published in the British media—e.g. by John Hatch[7]—cloaked an adroit and calculating political animal. From his own account, however, Kaunda led the struggle for independence at least with consummate idealism—and with Gandhian restraint:

> Succumbing to oppression is undignified and unworthy of any self-respecting man. On the other hand, open revolt often leads to the killing of countless people, those very people for whom freedom is sought. So we resort to the third method—the method of passive resistance or non-violent methods plus positive action. It is easy to succumb to oppression and grumble silently. It is, of course, less difficult to organize an open revolt, but it is more difficult to organize a non-violent struggle in that it calls for conviction on the part of all participants. This type of movement obviously calls for extensive coaching and very often results come after a long time, and this needs more discipline than open revolt. But the fruits of this training stand the participants in good stead when they take over the reins of government.[8]

Kaunda may have nobly adopted such methods against the white settlers who comprised the government of the Central African Federation and against the British Crown itself. As we have noted above, he moved ruthlessly—albeit without violence—against rivals such as Nkumbula and Kapwepwe. But he was also ruthless in the face of other challenges. Zambia, finally facing the imminence of independence, found that not all of Northern Rhodesia wished to be amalgamated into the new Zambia. What was called Barotseland—now Western Province and the centre of the Lozi population, with long kingship traditions and thus a sense of autonomy and self-governance[9]—was itself a British protectorate within the larger protectorate of Northern Rhodesia and was made part of

[6] Tetani Mwansah, 'Remembering Simon Kapwepwe 4 decades later', *Zambia Daily Mail*, 27 January 2020. Goodwin B. Mwangilwa, *The Kapwepwe Diaries*, Lusaka: Multimedia, 1986. Miles Larmer, *Rethinking African Politics: A History of Opposition in Zambia*, London: Routledge, 2016, Chapter 3.

[7] John Hatch, *Two African Statesmen: Kaunda of Zambia and Nyerere of Tanazania*, London: Secker & Warburg, 1976.

[8] Kaunda, *Zambia Shall be Free*, p 153.

[9] Akashambatwa Mbikusita-Lewanika, *King Lewanika I of Barotseland 1842–1916*, Lusaka, 2017 (as far as we can gather, this was a self-published document).

Zambia upon Zambia's independence in 1964. What was called the 'Barotseland Agreement' was meant to guarantee its autonomy, even as a Zambian province. To this day, there is festering discontent that the agreement was never honoured.[10] Indeed, shortly after independence, Kaunda began abrogating various provisions of the agreement and, in 1969, his parliament annulled the agreement altogether. Whether an independent Lozi state could survive on its own in a difficult world is an open question, but in his determination to build a single unified nation, Kaunda acted swiftly and, again, ruthlessly. And it was action of a more violent kind in the face of the rebellion of Alice Lenshina.

Described by her followers and indeed styled by herself as a prophetess, Lenshina—the Bemba rendition of Regina, or queen—was a staunch member of the Church of Scotland in Chinsali, to the north of Northern Rhodesia. After suffering serious cerebral malaria and recovering, she claimed a vision of Christ appeared to her in her coma and essentially instructed her to purify his teachings in her land. This meant a campaign not only against witchcraft but against the rival Catholic Church. She also began seeking converts from the Church of Scotland itself. By the end of the 1950s, her new Lumpa Church had 150,000 members and was itself a political force.[11] It sided with Harry Nkumbula's African National Congress, and when that organisation split, the Lumpa found itself at odds with Kaunda's UNIP. In 1964, just before independence, a fierce gun battle erupted between the two. And 1000 people died and 15,000 Lumpa members fled to Congo. Many never returned. Kaunda decreed a state of emergency, banned the church, arrested Lenshina; and she died, still under house arrest in 1978.

But her church had certain high moral teachings. It was against polygamy and was in favour of female upliftment. It was curiously proto-feminist.[12] And it seems Lenshina herself never wanted a firefight with UNIP, wishing to concentrate upon her moral teachings.[13] But, as a

[10] https://www.bbc.co.uk/news/world-africa-17546620
https://www.youtube.com/watch?v=M-ZYQKZzfVA 29 March 2012 and 20 July 2018, respectively.

[11] Andrew Roberts, *The Lumpa Church of Alice Lenshina*, Lusaka: Oxford University Press, 1972.

[12] Jonathan Kangwa, 'Prophecy, Divination and Gender Justice in the Lumpa Church in Zambia', *Feminist Theology*, 27:1, 2018, pp. 75–92.

[13] John Hudson, *A Time to Mourn: A personal account of the Lumpa Church revolt in Zambia*, Lusaka: Bookworld, 1999.

perceived political force or potential political force, and certainly one that had sided with Nkumbula, it was a point of focus for what has to be called a narrow-minded Kaunda. The public role of the Lumpa was not unlike that of many other churches in Africa, where capacity for organisation automatically implied political capacity in a continent where political parties were new and themselves establishing national and regional structures.[14] Antecedent and parallel structures were a threat.

If Kaunda dealt violently and ruthlessly with Lenshina and the Lumpa, it prefigured how he dealt with a slightly later rebellion, that of Adamson Mushala. The interesting aspect of the saga of Mushala, who professed a sort of Robin Hood vocation on the side of the poor,[15] but who also beguiled his supporters with reputed magical capacities, was that—supposedly under the auspices of Kaunda's UNIP—he was sent to China to learn guerrilla warfare to be used in the struggle for independence. But this is at odds with the Kaunda who professed non-violence, and it is often thought that the time it took to suppress his rebellion was because Mushala had embarrassing information about the early Kaunda and UNIP.[16] He returned from China too late to fight. Zambia had become independent. When Kaunda refused him a post in government, he took to the bush and launched a rebellion—but not before undergoing further training at the hands of the South Africans then occupying what is now Namibia, and from the Angolan rebel leader, Jonas Savimbi, himself also beholden to the South Africans.[17] His rebellion consisted not so much in fielding an army; it was more a band, perhaps a gang, of about two dozen members. Although hugely outgunned by government forces, they refused to surrender and conducted their rebellion from 1975 onwards. Why the government forces could not capture him is the question that has generated theories as to the early relationship between him and Kaunda. When he was finally killed in a firefight in 1982, the government went to great lengths to parade and televise his mutilated body as evidence the rebellion had finally ended. In fact, it hadn't. His last followers refused to surrender

[14] Paul Gifford, *African Christianity: Its Public Role*, London: Hurst, 1998.

[15] https://www.nytimes.com/1983/01/02/world/robin-hood-of-zambians-end-of-a-myth.html 2 January 1983.

[16] Patrick Wele, *Kaunda and Mushala Rebellion*, Lusaka: Multimedia, 1987.

[17] For two very different views, see Fred Bridgland, *Jonas Savimbi: A Key to Africa*, N.Y.: Paragon, 1987; and for the vicious context in which Savimbi was only a part, Stephen Chan, *Exporting Apartheid: Foreign Policies in Southern Africa 1978–1988*, N.Y.: St. Martins, 1990, pp. 47–65.

till 1990. But Zambia had become a one-party state in December 1972. Even dissent within the single party was crushed, as in the case of Simon Kapwepwe's doomed leadership bid against Kaunda in 1978. In a way, the saga of Mushala is the saga of the only possible opposition in a nation struggling to impose a single vision of political coherence.[18]

It was also a nation struggling to own its own resources, and a nation suddenly besieged by minority-ruled white nations to the south, east and west (Portuguese-ruled Angola and South African-ruled South West Africa [Namibia] to the west, Portuguese-ruled Mozambique to the east, and Southern Rhodesia and Apartheid South Africa to the south). The seizure of power by white settlers in Southern Rhodesia in 1965, just a year after Zambian independence, immediately presented a militarised threat to Kaunda's new nation. But, even before then, the question of ownership of the mines, in a country almost totally dependent on copper exports, was of huge importance.

These mines were owned by the British South Africa Company, a derivative of Cecil Rhodes's form of corporate colonialism, sanctioned and encouraged by the British Government, with financial rewards to it by way of resulting business monopolies linked to Great Britain that were established before rival efforts by enterprises linked to Portugal or other countries could take root; in turn, Rhodes secured British governmental protection for his enterprises with the formation of colonial structures literally called 'protectorates'. In the protectorate of Northern Rhodesia, the British South Africa Company owned the mines. Some of these had been acquired by way of concessions negotiated with local rulers—as was the case in Barotseland.

Talks leading to independence devoted much time to the question of mine ownership. It had not been fully resolved even on the eve of independence. Originally, mine royalties were to devolve to Zambia as late as 1986, but Kaunda's government wanted them from the moment of independence. Finally, this happened. Compensation had to be paid to both the company and Britain. Compromise formulae had been advanced before the company's capitulation to the demands of independence. One had been for Zambian ownership of mining assets, but with the continuation of existing operational arrangements under management contracts. Guy Scott recalls a taunt from white mine owners and workers: 'Lo Zambia ena kawena; lo mali ena katina.' This was in a creole, sometimes called

[18] Miles Larmer, *Rethinking African Politics*, Chapter 4.

Chilapalapa, 'kitchen speak' as a means of looking down on black employees, fit only to work in kitchens or other lowly jobs, by white bosses. It meant, 'Zambia is yours. The money is ours.'[19] But taking full control of the mines also meant the need to manage them along modern and productive lines—and there were the mounting demands of the mine workers for increased salaries, as well as an influx of workers from surrounding countries looking for work in the mines. The new government also had to learn modern labour relations in the face of demands for a minimum wage which the country could not have afforded.

The nationalisation of the mines brought a whole host of technical problems. Oliver Saasa writes about the balance of ratios to do with local content, imported content, management and diversification. None of it was free of technocratic considerations, planning skills and high risks in catering for an international market.[20]

Salaries for mine workers were not the only problem. Salaries in the civil service to encourage high standards of public administration were something dealt with by people like John Mwanakatwe—who described the frustrations of trying to be fair, encouraging and not spendthrift in a new climate of independent possibility.[21] Independence thus came with literal costs—but none more so than those associated with revolt in Southern Rhodesia in 1965.

Not a protectorate, but given a large degree of self-government, Southern Rhodesia was still ostensibly subject to the Crown. In a following chapter, we deal with the politics and the literature of the period. For now, the observation is simply that all road and rail infrastructure had been built by Cecil Rhodes and the British South Africa Company. They went south from Zambia, through Southern Rhodesia—with its name abbreviated upon the illegal Unilateral Declaration of Independence in 1965 to simply 'Rhodesia'. The products of the mines could only be exported through white territory. Rhodesia had defied the Crown and rejected independence with black majority rule. It could hold the newly independent black-majority-ruled state of Zambia to economic ransom,

[19] Guy Scott, *Adventures in African Politics: A Story in Black & White*, Boulder: Lynne Rienner, 2019, Chapter 3.

[20] Oliver S. Saasa, 'Determinants of Zambia's Policies towards the Mining Industry: 1964–1984', in Kwaku Osei-Hwedie and Muna Ndulo (eds.), *Issues in Zambian Development*, Roxbury: Omenana, 1985.

[21] John Mwankatwe, *Teacher, Politician, Lawyer: My Autobiography*, Lusaka: Bookworld, 2003, Chapter 9.

and even if not Rhodesia, Apartheid South Africa—where the transport links continued until they reached South African ports—could squeeze Zambia even more. A great deal of the manufactures that Zambia had to import in order to establish modern development and modern lifestyles not only came through South Africa but were made in South Africa.

From an early stage South Africa made it clear, it would support white-ruled Rhodesia. Certainly, it provided a lifeline for the country against Harold Wilson's economic sanctions. The same transport routes to Rhodesia from South Africa continued on to Zambia. And, as tensions grew and liberation movements became militant and themselves militarised, Zambia found itself in a literal frontline. Even if only as a modest deterrent, Kaunda needed to field a Zambian army[22] and a Zambian airforce.[23] The doctrine of pacific resistance was extended by Kaunda to Zambia's relationships with the white south. Militarily defeating ragtag rebel movements was one thing, but taking on modern armies something else entirely. All the while Kaunda played a huge brinksmanship by hosting in Lusaka and elsewhere in Zambia liberation movements working for majority rule in Rhodesia, South West Africa and South Africa itself. But, even if his military forces were sparsely used—and more of that later—they still required training, not just to be soldiers in any non-technocratic sense but, especially with the airforce, to be able to use modern equipment of a sophisticated sort. By the 1980s, figures like the brilliant airforce commander, General Hananiah Lungu, cut dashing technocratic figures—Lungu taking delight in alarming manufacturers at international military airshows by asking to test their planes himself[24]—but someone like him was the product of an educational infrastructure that Kaunda had to begin, almost from scratch, putting into place. For, at independence, Zambia was a sparse country in terms of educated people of any description.

In 1964 Zambia entered nation-statehood with a total of 109 university graduates. Only 0.5% of the population had completed primary school.[25] But it wasn't just a case of building a national university,[26] and

[22] https://www.globalsecurity.org/military/world/africa/zm-army.htm

[23] https://www.globalsecurity.org/military/world/africa/zm-af.htm

[24] From discussions between Stephen Chan and General Hananiah Lungu in the 1980s.

[25] Yuyi K. Libakeni, *They built Zambia: Zambia's hundred graduates at independence*, Lusaka: Y.K. Libakeni, 2008.

[26] Sitwe Benson Mkadawire, *Higher Education Systems and Institutions: Zambia*, Dordrecht: Springer, 2018. For a brief summary: https://www.unza.zm/about/history and https://www.unza.zm/international/?p=history

getting children to complete school, it was in the words of the early Cabinet Minister, John Mwanakatwe, a question of 'desegregation of schools'.[27] By this he meant the desegregation of provision, whereby schools for non-black students were differently provided and financed. Peter Snelson, in his own authoritative account, pays tribute to what Mwanakatwe did as Minister of Education.[28] Snelson was in no doubt that it was a transformative, almost revolutionary step, not only to expand educational provision but to equalise it—with the aim of equalising it a high level and in the face of white objections that the education of their own children would suffer in what they expected would be an equalisation downwards.

In this milieu, as Zambia began to contemplate and engage with what independence entailed—and what modernity it unavoidably entailed—the public imagination was one precisely of independent development equating with modernity.[29] It was not an imagination bereft of international comparators. The stirrings of Asia economies and societies were an example. In the range of modern examples, the Soviets had launched their first Sputnik satellite only seven years earlier, in 1957. In 1960, John F. Kennedy, who was greeted as an inspirational figure at that time, declared the need to close the gap with the Soviets in the space race. It was a matter both of dignity in not being behind and also one of technological idealism. But in 1961, it was the Soviets who launched Yuri Gagarin into orbit. The USA got their own John Glenn into space in 1962. From 1963, the race to reach the moon was launched, with both the USA and the Soviet Union publicly committed to reaching this new frontier.[30] It was this kind of aspiration, this sense of a race for the highest levels of modernity and human achievement, that reached Zambia also—as it, not just within political idealism, entered its new age. Building towards this moment, even without educational background—for that had been largely impossible—there was the most modern of aspirations. 'Quaintly modern' might be a genteel pejorative but a condescending one all the same. Given

[27] Mwanakatwe, *Teacher, Politician, Lawyer: My Autobiography*, the title of Chapter 7.

[28] Peter Desmond Snelson, *To Independence and Beyond: Memoirs of a Colonial Commonwealth*, London: Radcliffe, 1993. Chapters 4 and 5.

[29] James Ferguson, *Expectations of Modernity: Myths and Meaning on the Zambian Copperbelt*, Berkeley: University of California Press, 1999.

[30] See James Donovan, *Shoot for the Moon: The Space Race and the Extraordinary Voyage of Apollo 11*, London: Little Brown, 2019; Matthew Brezinski, *Red Moon Rising*, London: Bloomsbury, 2008.

the turmoil and challenges confronting what many have regarded as a model achievement of independence—without huge violence against the colonial authorities and white population (although, as in the Mushala case, this may once have been contemplated)—given the compression of time in which the new government wished to 'make it', ruthlessly if need be to achieve unity and development, the atmosphere of public life in Zambia in 1964 was such that perhaps it would have been surprising if there had not been a brief flurry to enter the space race, to reach for the moon and the stars.

At the end of 1964 Kaunda set off on an international tour. It was then one of the longest trips ever made by an African leader. It was to 'put Zambia on the map', but not with other African states. He visited mostly modern states, including the USA and the Soviet Union. His developing philosophy of 'Humanism', which we shall discuss later, was predicated on the ostensible equality of human beings. And perhaps this was the properly naïve aspect of early Zambia—not a foray into the space race but a foray predicated on the ostensible equality of nations in which Zambia sought to deport itself as a recognisable compatriot of the greatest powers on earth.

CHAPTER 2

Imagining Independence

Abstract Independence was followed immediately by the refusal of Rhodesia to the south to accept its own independence on the basis of majority rule. The white settlers declared a unilateral independence on their own racist terms and prepared to defend it militarily. Zambia had no military resources and had to develop them from scratch, even while President Kaunda advanced a philosophy of pacifism and what he called 'Humanism'.

Keywords White rebellion • Sanctions • Mediation • Philosopher king • Commonwealth

As Zambia attained independence and Zambians were imagining what the fruits of independence would be, they were also mindful that the long build-up to white rebellion in Southern Rhodesia could erupt into outright rejection both of the Crown and the black majority. Harold Macmillan's great speech in 1960 about the 'wind of change', delivered in the South African Parliament, had fallen on deaf ears both in South Africa and Southern Rhodesia.[1] If the white minority in Southern Rhodesia was

[1] https://web-archives.univ-pau.fr/english/TD2doc1.pdf
https://www.youtube.com/watch?v=c07MiYfpOMw

S. Chan, *The Economic Transformation and Political Economy of Zambia*, Palgrave Studies in African and Development Economics,
https://doi.org/10.1007/978-3-031-93030-0_2

obdurate in its sense of superiority and sought immunity from black rule, the black nationalist movement was splintered and its factions feuded—not only in Southern Rhodesia but within Zambia. In 1964, UNIP withdrew its support from ZANU (Zimbabwe African National Union—later to be led by Robert Mugabe) and threw its weight behind Joshua Nkomo's ZAPU (Zimbabwe African People's Union). This would later bring Zambia into Cold War politics, as ZAPU secured support from the Soviet Union and established its military bases on Zambian soil. Its soldiers were trained and equipped by Soviet advisers, and while this was done with discretion and away from the urban centres, the idea of African rebellion in military uniform entered the public imagination. The Victoria Falls (the *Mosi o Tunya*, the Thundering Smoke) which marked the border between Zambia and the western part of Southern Rhodesia—Nkomo's heartland and where his army later conducted the bulk of their operations—became figuratively the point of transition of a new country seeking peace and development to one engaged in confrontation. Zambia had to imagine both what its own independence would bring and its role in bringing legitimate independence to its southern neighbour. In 1965, the year after Zambian independence, Southern Rhodesia announced its Unilateral Declaration of Independence (UDI) and broke away from the British Crown.

It had not been a straight line towards this rupture. Earlier white leaders such as Garfield Todd had sought to inculcate a liberal set of policies towards the African population.[2] But when UDI came, it expressed a curious white nationalism. Dependent on support from Apartheid South Africa, it did not contemplate any union with the larger country. If it had undertaken union, the struggle against white rule would have been much harder both for the nationalist parties and their armies, and for Zambia. It was hard enough in any case for Zambia. There was always a certain Zambian rue that the Rhodesians might get away with their rebellion. The bruised feeling was that during the days of Federation, the proceeds from Northern Rhodesian mines had been diverted southwards and had built a formidable manufacturing capacity in Southern Rhodesia. Even without UDI, the imbalance in manufacturing capacity would have been great.

[2] Susan Woodhouse, *Garfield Todd: The End of the Liberal Dream in Rhodesia*, Harare: Weaver, 2018.

https://www.theguardian.com/news/2002/oct/14/guardianobituaries.obituaries1 14 October 2002.

'We were dependent', Guy Scott wrote, 'upon our southern neighbours for the supply of the most basic commodities.' But with UDI and British Prime Minister Harold Wilson's economic sanctions on the white regime, followed by UN sanctions, 'Rhodesia ... retaliated by imposing them in turn on us. The joke of the time,' according to Scott, 'was "Sanctions are finally biting; Zambia is on its knees." We were short of fuel, cement, a range of foodstuffs, even maize.' Scott even maintained that without the pillage of the north by the south during Confederation, and the resources and capacities gained, UDI would not have lasted more than a few months.[3]

Economic sanctions had been imposed by the British Government as the first (and really the only) resort towards ending the rebellion. Britain was very short of money. The Wilson Government was on a perilous descending path towards what became, within ten years, the strictures of the International Monetary Fund (IMF) and devaluation,[4] and the plan drawn up by British defence chiefs and military planners to end UDI by force was deemed too risky and, above all, too expensive.[5] What seemed to be a timid response to rebellion was occasioned by some sense certainly of kinship with white settlers who had migrated to Rhodesia from Britain, the whole 'kith and kin' perception, but also upon empty coffers. Wilson took a very great deal of international criticism for his seeming timidity.[6] But this timidity was in fact extreme. Carl Watts, in his archival research in several countries, documented the episode when the white Rhodesian security and military chiefs, understanding that UDI was in fact a treasonous act against the Crown, offered to arrest Ian Smith; but the British Governor, Sir Humphrey Gibbs, although himself an opponent of UDI, feared a *coup d'etat* by other officers, with a consequent blood bath, and declined the offer.[7] He no doubt had also in mind that the British Government would not militarily stand by him in such a situation.

[3] Guy Scott, *Adventures in Zambian* Politics, Chapter Three.

[4] https://www.nationalarchives.gov.uk/cabinetpapers/themes/sterling-devalued-imf-loan.htm

https://www.nationalarchives.gov.uk/cabinetpapers/themes/imf-crisis.htm

[5] https://www.independent.co.uk/news/military-chiefs-reviewed-plan-to-invade-rhodesia-1321929.html

[6] Paul Foot, *The Politics of Harold Wilson*, Harmondsworth: Penguin, 1968, Chapter 8.

[7] Carl Peter Watts, *Rhodesia's Unilateral Declaration of Independence: An International History*, Houndmills: Palgrave, 2012, p 60.

This situation led to an acceptance in Zambia that military options rested with the nationalist movements in Rhodesia and, upon their being outlawed there, it was the duty of Zambia to host them. But the choice to prioritise support to Joshua Nkomo's ZAPU as opposed to ZANU was a complex one. Joshua Nkomo had been imprisoned in Rhodesia in 1964. ZANU was then led by Ndabaningi Sithole, who was however also in a Rhodesian prison. His book on African nationalism[8] had inflamed the white minority leaders of Rhodesia and five years after its publication he was imprisoned. This was again in 1964, a year before UDI. In fact, the imprisonment of these leaders was taken as an indicator in the region that a white rebellion against the Crown was imminent. Also in a Rhodesian prison from 1963 was the ZANU secretary-General Robert Mugabe. In the absence of Mugabe and Sithole, Herbert Chitepo led ZANU from his residence in Lusaka. But all three ZANU leaders were affronted by Joshua Nkomo's apparent willingness to contemplate a compromise with the Ian Smith Rhodesia Front party that led the push to UDI. Bickering on Zambian soil between the exiled Zimbabwean groups became intense. Kaunda sought to reduce the scope of their activities and size of their exile offices, but to no avail. When, in 1974, Sithole and Nkomo were released, Sithole had already faced a leadership challenge from Mugabe as he had renounced violence while in prison. When Mugabe was himself released in 1975, he made his way by bizarre circumstances to Mozambique, via Zambia. He had first gone to Zambia, only promptly to be imprisoned by Kaunda—who saw him as bent on violence that would be uncontrollable by Zambia—but was then, almost certainly with Zambian connivance, spirited to Mozambique to avoid further embarrassment on Zambian soil—where he was promptly put under a form of house arrest by President Samora Machel. This left Nkomo heading ZAPU in Zambia after he also had made his way there. Herbert Chitepo was assassinated by a car bomb in Lusaka in 1975,[9] and a huge controversy erupted, which has lasted till this day, as to who was to blame. Chitepo had, before his death, done much to publicise the cause of majority rule—even making a well-received lecture tour as far away as New Zealand.[10] But this left Mugabe to direct what was now a commitment to war, after winning the trust of Machel,

[8] Ndabaningi Sithole, *African Nationalism*, Cape Town: Oxford University Press, 1959.

[9] Luise White, *The Assassination of Herbert Chitepo: Texts and Politics in Zimbabwe*, Bloomington: Indiana University Press, 2003.

[10] Stephen Chan, as the national student president in New Zealand, was his official host.

from Mozambique. Nkomo's ZAPU also prepared for war. But the preparations of the two parties were very different. Kaunda was probably relieved that ZANU had departed, one way or another, from Zambian soil. But the style of ZAPU's preparation for war probably also appealed. Whereas Mugabe secured Chinese assistance for a guerrilla war, which he conducted from Mozambican bases to the east of Rhodesia, Nkomo secured Soviet support for his thrust southwards into western Rhodesia from Zambia. There were tanks, armoured personnel carriers, artillery, even a small number of Mikoyan MIG fighter jets. Almost none of this equipment was actually used in battle. Both guerrilla armies fought on a denial-of-control basis—not so much, despite propaganda, to 'liberate' territory, as to make it impossible for the white government to control in any secure or lasting manner large segments of the countryside. Particularly on the ZAPU side, war was more a chess game of positioning, withdrawal and repositioning than full-scale conflict.[11] Mugabe's army accused Nkomo's of not actually having fought tooth and claw. But, for Kaunda's Zambia, Nkomo's army had all the parade ground features at least of modernity. And the ZAPU army (named ZIPRA—Zimbabwe People's Revolutionary Army) had sufficient real technology to shoot down a passenger plane in the latter part of 1978. They shot down a second craft in 1979, in the mistaken belief that the Rhodesian military chief, Peter Walls, was on board.[12] What they used was a Soviet-made Strela-2 surface-to-air infrared homing missile, more commonly known as a SAM 7, a shoulder-mounted weapon. ZIPRA forces also tried to shoot down a South African Airways flight carrying President P.W. Botha, but failed to do so.[13]

Mugabe's ZANLA (Zimbabwe African National Liberation Army) were never able to attempt such feats. Armed primarily with AK47s, these were supplemented by light Soviet machine guns, the PKM and RPD;

[11] Stephen Chan's discussions with Rhodesian Brigadiers commanding the 'sub-JOCS' in western Zimbabwe, the regional outposts of the Rhodesian Joint Operational Command, during the January to March 1980 ceasefire. Chan anchored the Commonwealth Observer Group in Matabeleland North and Matabeleland South during the ceasefire and the transition from armed struggle to elections—which Mugabe's party won.

[12] https://www.nytimes.com/1979/02/13/archives/all-59-die-on-rhodesia-airliner-shot-down-by-missile-top-general-on.html 13 February 1979.

https://www.youtube.com/watch?v=EbxMO5awVXM

[13] Elakim Sibanda, *The Zimbabwe African People's Union, 1961–87: A Political History*, Trenton: Africa World Press, 2005, p 192.

together with some recoilless rifles, mortars and anti-tank grenade launchers secured from the international arms bazaar.[14]

Military modernity however made its appearance in Zambia as early as 1965, shortly after UDI. With Zambia facing threats by Rhodesian warplanes against the electricity supplies for the copper mines on the Zambian Copperbelt, the UK despatched a squadron of Javelin aircraft as a defensive shield.[15] These were interceptor aircraft—not ideally suited for direct ground attacks and intended as a deterrent rather than a fighting force. They also constituted an inducement to Zambia not to ally itself too closely to foreign powers like the Soviet Union. Britain was far from ready still to enter a military fray, but the symbolism of the Javelin squadron was a relatively cheap price for Harold Wilson to pay to maintain influence in emerging Africa and, having paraded the symbol, he withdrew the squadron in 1966, but the low flypasts and displays the aircraft made over Zambian cities impressed everyone.[16]

Modernity however cannot banish the terrors and traumas of war. Even with the wish to fight a war of territorial denial, engagement was inevitable. In the Zimbabwean novels that deal with the war, it was clear that all sides suffered—from the white Rhodesian soldiers and conscripts,[17] to the guerrilla forces—whether serving Mugabe[18] or Nkomo's[19] vision of liberation. The trauma was immense.[20] All cultural means were used to aid the guerrillas' war efforts, including recourse to spirit mediums.[21] On the Rhodesian side, recourse to mercenaries, including many US soldiers of fortune, bulked up the embattled conscripts. Many of the mercenaries

[14] Paul Moorcraft, *Mugabe's War Machine: Saving or Savaging Zimbabwe?*, Barnsley: Pen & Sword Military, 2011, p 69.

[15] https://www.youtube.com/watch?v=ojKYro2VuTk

https://api.parliament.uk/historic-hansard/commons/1965/dec/01/zambia-british-forces-and-rhodesia

[16] https://www.key.aero/forum/historic-aviation/126480-gloster-javelins-zambia-1966

[17] Angus Shaw, *Kandaya: Another Time, Another Place*, Harare: Baobab, 1993.

[18] Alexander Kanengoni, *Echoing Silences*, Harare: Baobab, 1993.

[19] Yvonne Vera, *The Stone Virgins*, Harare: weaver, 2002.

[20] Stephen Chan, 'The Memory of Violence: trauma in the writings of Alexander Kanengoni and Yvonne Vera and the idea of unreconciled citizenship in Zimbabwe', *Third World Quarterly*, 26:2, 2005, pp. 369–382.

[21] Terence Ranger, *Peasant Consciousness and Guerrilla War in Zimbabwe*, London: James Currey, 1985; David Lan, *Guns and Rain*, London: James Currey, 1985; Billy Mukamuri, *Making Sense of Social Forestry: A Political and Contextual Study of Forestry Practice in South Central Zimbabwe*, Tampere: Acta Universitatis Tamperensis, 1995.

were psychotic and themselves traumatised from previous wars, and many fought while high on drugs, and many committed gratuitous atrocities.[22] And, of course, Rhodesia required a huge amount of South African support. This was sometimes in terms of personnel as much as equipment.[23]

All this left Kaunda as leader of the freshly minted Zambia in an invidious position. He did not have sufficient military resources to take the fight to Rhodesia, especially a Rhodesia able to be reinforced by South Africa. He regarded it, and was supported by his electorate, as a principle that he should support the cause of liberation. He chose a particular side in the liberation struggle in the neighbouring country and hosted a foreign rebel army on his soil. Symbolic British support flew by like a flash in the pan. All his economy depended on transport routes that ran through white-ruled territory. The governments of Rhodesia and South Africa had leverage over him. He had to walk a diplomatic tightrope. Zambian development slowed down and the anticipated fruits of independence never came. Richard Hall called it the 'high price of principles'.[24] Rhodesian commando raids came and went. One tried to assassinate Joshua Nkomo and succeeded in leaving his Lusaka house a smouldering ruin.[25] Nkomo's account was that he escaped through the toilet window—although, given his girth, the improbability of this became a Zambian joke. There would seem to have been a British intelligence warning that a 'hit squad' was on the way.[26] Even so, a year later, when one of the current authors went to live in Zambia, the ruined house had become a tourist attraction and the joking speculation was always about how the rotund Nkomo had squeezed through the toilet window, whether he had to stand on the toilet seat, whether as a result the toilet seat had collapsed and Nkomo's foot had had to find purchase in his own faeces. The high price of principles had not incapacitated coprophagic satire.

South Africa, however, for its part had no wish for full-scale war. In an effort at *détente* with what were now commonly referred to as the front-line states—Zambia being a particular target for South African

[22] Gerald Horne, *From the Barrel of a Gun: The United States and the War against Zimbabwe, 1965–1980*, Chapel Hill: University of North Carolina Press, 2001, p 211.

[23] Paul Moorcraft, *Mugabe's War Machine: Saving or Savaging Zimbabwe?*, Chapter 3.

[24] Richard Hall, *The High Price of Principles: Kaunda and the White South*, London: Hodder & Stoughton, 1969.

[25] https://www.nytimes.com/1979/04/14/archives/rhodesians-strike-at-zambian-capital-in-bid-to-get-nkomo-rebels-in.html 14 April 1979.

[26] https://www.bbc.co.uk/news/world-africa-14311834

overtures—seeking to reduce violence to 'manageable proportions' and preserve the key national interests of South Africa, Rhodesia and Zambia, South Africa's President B. J. Vorster persuaded Kaunda to co-host talks in 1975 between Ian Smith's government and the various nationalist and guerrilla factions. After much bickering, a compromise venue was found and that was on the Victoria Falls Bridge, a railway carriage substituting for a conference room, with a white line painted at its halfway point—marking the exact border of Rhodesia and Zambia over which the carriage was parked. Vorster and Smith sat on one side, Kaunda and the nationalist leaders on the other.

The Victoria Falls conference produced no result.[27] However, it reinforced Kaunda's image of pacific and mediatory commitment—not only in terms of conflict in Rhodesia, for Kaunda and Vorster had private discussions about a range of Southern African issues.[28] In fact, the conference gave the guerrilla armies time to regroup after suffering setbacks to their fledgling operations at the hands of Rhodesian forces in 1974. Fighting intensified after the conference—but the talks did set into train continual efforts at negotiation. The parties met again in Geneva in 1976.[29] Again, no peaceful outcome was achieved.[30] Mediatory efforts were renewed, the most well-known being the Anglo-American initiative that began in 1977 involving Andrew Young and David Owen. Again, it had no successful outcome.[31] It was the Lusaka Commonwealth Heads of Government

[27] http://news.bbc.co.uk/onthisday/hi/dates/stories/august/26/newsid_2535000/2535825.stm 26 August 1975.

[28] https://www.nytimes.com/1975/08/26/archives/2-rhodesian-sides-confer-into-night-at-victoria-falls-vorster-of.html 26 August 1975.

[29] http://www.colonialfilm.org.uk/node/2574

[30] https://www.nytimes.com/1976/10/25/archives/disputes-on-rhodesia-plan-persist-as-leaders-gather-for-geneva-talk.html 25 October 1976. https://www.nytimes.com/1976/10/29/archives/geneva-talks-on-rhodesia-open-after-chairman-averts-a-boycott.html 29 October 1976.

https://api.parliament.uk/historic-hansard/commons/1976/nov/17/rhodesia-geneva-conference-1 17 November 1976.

https://api.parliament.uk/historic-hansard/lords/1976/dec/14/rhodesia-geneva-conference 14 December 1976.

[31] Elaine Windrich, 'The Anglo-American Initiative on Rhodesia: An Interim Assessment', *The World Today*, 35:7, July 1979, pp. 294–305.

https://api.parliament.uk/historic-hansard/lords/1977/jul/25/rhodesia-anglo-american-policy-1 25 July 1977.

https://www.nytimes.com/1978/05/29/archives/south-african-leader-rejects-wests-rhodesia-plan-vorsters-position.html 29 May 1978.

Meeting that finally brokered a breakthrough. Chaired by Kaunda, and involving efforts from an unlikely combination of personalities, this will be considered below. But, in all the years of war and fruitless talks, the position of Zambia was unenviable.

Kaunda travelled widely to propagate the need for help to Zambia. His reputation as a wise and thoughtful leader would precede him, especially as by the 1970s his 'philosophy' of 'Humanism' had won him much respect for its seeming idealism and faith in humane principles. Simultaneously Christian and socialist, while claiming African antecedents for its sense of equal justice for all, its face value was attractive.[32] Indeed, it was propagated as the guiding national philosophy of state in 1967, very shortly after both Zambian independence and Rhodesian UDI. Its seeming disdain for violence also earned him, in addition to John Hatch's accolade of 'philosopher king', the descriptor 'African Gandhi'.[33] This kind of reputation was why, on his visit to China in 1974, the Chinese announced that Mao's Three World Theory—ostensibly an operational doctrine that said that equality with the superpowers could be attained by third world solidarity, except this global equality would be effectively led by China—had been finalised after discussions between Mao and Kaunda. The wise and peaceful African lent the seal of moral approval to China's form of internationalism, but enunciated along 'Humanistic' lines of equal global justice.[34]

Where the payoff to Kaunda came was the Chinese effort from 1968 to 1976 to build a railway from Zambia to the Tanzanian port of Dar es Salaam. It was a massive project, 1860 km long, involving both Chinese and African labourers working side by side. It became part of the romantic Chinese sense of what internationalism entailed—and, indeed, was a self-justification of China to China that it was one with those who suffered.[35] It was meant to substitute at least in part for the rail routes running south from Zambia through Rhodesia and South Africa, but never attained sufficient capacity to fulfil that aim.

But the tightrope that Kaunda walked, advertising pacific resistance to the white south while engaged in international diplomacy to secure

[32] Kenneth D. Kaunda, *A Humanist in Africa*, London: Longman Green, 1966.

[33] https://www.nytimes.com/1962/04/18/archives/a-disciple-of-gandhi-kenneth-kaunda-son-of-a-missionary.html 18 April 1962.

[34] Stephen Chan, 'China's Foreign Policy and Africa: The Rise and Fall of China's Three World's Theory', *The Round Table*, 296, 1985, p 378.

[35] https://chineseposters.net/themes/tazara-railway.php

sufficient allies so that he would not have to withstand full-scale military attack, was almost an invitation to the Rhodesians to attack both guerrilla bases and Zambian infrastructure at will—with the proviso that the attacks were within some rough and ready sense of restraint—although not always; what was called Operation Gatling in 1978 lasted three days and killed 1500 ZIPRA soldiers and wounded another 1348 with 198 unaccounted for.[36] The sense of Rhodesian impunity was best exemplified during this operation by the conduct of its airforce. A wing of Hawker Hunters circled over Lusaka's airport and its commander, who identified himself as 'Green Leader', announced that their attack was against 'Rhodesian dissidents' and not Zambia. However, his Hawker Hunters would shoot down any Zambian fighter aircraft that dared to take off and challenge them. The Zambians complied.[37] The folklore relates that the exchange between Green Leader and the Lusaka control tower was extremely polite and cordial. The sense that no one had the courage to take off in challenge is, however, contested by Zambian airmen who insisted to one of the current authors that they had received orders directly from the President's office not to resist.

In his 1986 conversations in Lusaka with the late General Hananiah Lungu, Zambian airforce commander at the time of Operation Gatling, and later Minister of Defence, Stephen Chan directly questioned him about what happened then. To paraphrase the response, Zambian fighters had indeed been ordered by the President's State House not to challenge any aspect of the Rhodesian incursion. But many fighter pilots had wanted to do so. And, despite the cordial exchanges between Green Leader and the control tower, other Rhodesian pilots were mocking about the Zambian 'cowardice'. Incensed, Lungu himself afterwards took off in his own fighter plane, unaccompanied by any other planes, crossed into Rhodesia, and dropped smoke bombs the full length of the Rhodesian Airforce main runway—as a 'we could have taken you on if we had been allowed to' riposte—and flew home unpursued.

[36] Paul Moorcraft and Peter McLaughlin, *The Rhodesian War: A Military History*, Barnsley: Pen & Sword, 2008.

http://www.saha.org.za/zapu/rhodesian_attacks.htm

[37] https://christopherhepworth.com/war-strikes-home-devastating-1978-green-leader-raid-zambia/ 3 January 2018.

https://www.youtube.com/watch?v=dzJfy5z5gj4

https://www.youtube.com/watch?v=xYhir4aWEgA

Similarly, in 1979, as the war reached its zenith and with all sides seeking maximum advantage before rumours of peace talks could harden, Rhodesian planes began bombing Zambian infrastructure, including roads and bridges. University students were hastily recruited into defence brigades to reinforce the Zambian army. They were armed and deployed to guard the main bridges along the important roads. At one such deployment, one of Stephen Chan's students reported to him that they were ordered that they could under no account, except on the express orders of State House, return fire if they came under Rhodesian attack. Chan's student was elected by his detachment to give notice of disobedience. He marched forward from the assembled ranks, saluted the commanding officer, and said in clear almost strident tones, 'Sir! The men have instructed me to say to you, Sir! That in the event that we come under fire we shall by all means return fire. Sir!' If the war had continued, Kaunda might well have fallen off his tightrope. But, finally, in the latter part of 1979, in Lusaka itself, the beginnings of serious peace talks did begin to materialise.

It had been spurred by the coming to power in the UK of Margaret Thatcher in 1979. Determined to cut away the Rhodesian albatross from her country's neck, she declared she might move to recognise a compromise government involving Ian Smith and the most moderate of the nationalist leaders, Bishop Abel Muzorewa. She had not consulted her own Foreign Secretary, Lord Carrington, who knew instantly that the international community would not accept such an accommodation and that the UK would lose almost all its remaining purchase in the Commonwealth of Nations. Some felt the Commonwealth might have even broken up on this issue. As it was, a Commonwealth Heads of Government Meeting (CHOGM) was scheduled for the first week in August 1979 in Lusaka. This gave Carrington the early summer months in which to prepare alternative British positions. In his memoirs he is very diplomatic as to why he sought alternatives. He attributed no blame towards Thatcher, except to say he agreed with her that it was time to move on from the Rhodesia that had become a festering sore in British foreign policy.[38] The issue had become a constant cause of criticism and negative feeling towards Britain on the part of African governments and many other parts of the emerging world. Carrington despatched Lord Harlech and Sir Antony Duff to undertake intensive shuttle diplomacy among African capitals to discern what was the least position acceptable to

[38] Lord Carrington, *Reflect on Things Past*, London: Collins, 1988, p 288–292.

their governments. At the same time, Kaunda despatched Mark Chona on equally intensive shuttle diplomacy to agree a common African objection to the British inclination. The Commonwealth CHOGM was thus preceded by much diplomacy. One fly in the ointment was the very low opinion Carrington had of Kaunda. He recounts a meeting in which Edward Heath had chastised Kaunda on the Rhodesia issue, saying that Kaunda expected too much of Britain—to which Kaunda and his delegation began rolling their eyes, intoning 'My God, my God, how terrible, terrible' for several minutes. Carrington clearly found this ridiculous.[39] The strategic and tactical handling of the CHOGM thus fell to the Commonwealth Secretary-General, Shridath Ramphal, who persuaded Kaunda to chair the CHOGM in a particular extended way that would give Ramphal time to 'work' the British delegation.[40] He did this by having a queue of the most distinguished (people like Nyerere) and the most handsome (people like ex-fighter pilot Michael Manley of Jamaica) Commonwealth leaders pay courtesy calls on Thatcher, basically to charm her.[41] Australia's Malcolm Fraser also played this role while emphasising he too was a bedrock conservative figure—who all the same saw sense in a wider view on how to take the Rhodesia issue forwards.[42] Kaunda was deployed to add his own charm, and the images of his dancing with Thatcher at the gala ball of the summit meeting, after an outline agreement was achieved on the Rhodesian issue, shows a radiant couple.[43]

That agreement was to convene peace talks in London under Carrington's chairmanship. Kaunda was to persuade Joshua Nkomo to attend, Mozambique's Samora Machel was persuaded to ensure Mugabe attended, and the South Africans—understanding that the alternative was continued war and an increasing prospect of violence spreading into South Africa itself—ensured Smith and Muzorewa attended. As it was, the talks

[39] Carrington, *Reflect on Things Past*, pp. 254–5.

[40] Derek Ingram, 'Thatcher and Ramphal: A Long and Turbulent Relationship', *The Round Table*, 398, 2008, pp. 781–790.

[41] Stephen Chan, *The Commonwealth in World Politics: A Study of International Action 1965 to 1985*, London: Lester Crook, 1988, pp36–9.

[42] For his adroit diplomacy, see the record of Fraser's meeting with Thatcher and Carrington in Lusaka: https://c59574e9047e61130f13-3f71d0fe2b653c4f00f32175760e96e7.ssl.cf1.rackcdn.com/6A2FAEEB682E49C49547299B2A973C81.pdf and for Fraser's own account, Malcolm Fraser, *The Political Memoirs*, Carlton: Miegunyah Press, 2010, pp. 505–515.

[43] https://www.shutterstock.com/editorial/image-editorial/prime-minister-margaret-thatcher-and-kenneth-kaunda-zambian-president-dancing-lusaka-zambia-5948204a

were timely in more ways than one. A stalemate had been forced on the battlefield, and hostilities would thereafter be acts of attrition in which, by sheer force of numbers, white Rhodesia would be ground down long before the Guerrilla armies. It had been a very long and arduous struggle.[44] For Carrington it was also another chance for the UK to rid itself of the Rhodesian albatross and he set himself to be the steely chairman, driving the process ruthlessly forward. Davidow described the negotiations, conducted in London's Lancaster House, in detail.[45] Newhouse captured the personal cost to Carrington and his musings during the difficult talks.[46] But he drove the talks with what seemed often to the participants—being played off one faction against the other—unfair tactics. On more than one occasion, the guerrilla factions, negotiating under a common rubric and name, the Patriotic Front (PF), felt like walking out. Ramphal restrained them and advised them and often had Kaunda or Machel on the other end of the telephone line waiting to speak to Nkomo or Mugabe as they walked into his office at Marlborough House, one small block from Lancaster House.[47]

That the Lancaster House talks succeeded probably owed as much to Ramphal as to Carrington, and January to March 1980 was set as a transition period during which the hitherto banned nationalist movements were free to re-enter the country to campaign in a majority-rule election, and their guerrilla forces were also to assemble in ceasefire camps. All of this was meant to be superintended by a new British Governor and observed internationally. That it all went well was as much by good luck as good management. Stephen Chan, together with Emmanuel Apea, anchored the western provinces of Matabeleland North and Matabeleland South for the Commonwealth observation of the electoral and ceasefire processes.[48] These were the provinces of greatest activity on the part of Joshua Nkomo's ZIPRA guerrillas, and Matabeleland North was divided from Zambia by the Victoria Falls, the symbolic point of struggle and disillusionment in Dominic Mulaisho's great novel, *The Smoke That Thunders*. This novel

[44] Anthony Verrier, *The Road to Zimbabwe 1890–1980*, London: Jonathan Cape, 1986.

[45] Jeffrey Davidow, *A Peace in Southern Africa—The Lancaster House Conference on Rhodesia, 1979*, Boulder: Westview, 1984.

[46] https://www.newyorker.com/magazine/1983/02/14/a-sense-of-duty 7 February 1983.

[47] Stephen Chan himself once had to escort Joshua Nkomo to Ramphal's office.

[48] Stephen Chan, *The Commonwealth Observer Group in Zimbabwe: A Personal Memoir*, Gweru: Mambo Press, 1985.

was published in 1979, shortly before the end of war in Rhodesia. Mulaisho's backdrop was informed by all the years of struggle that had preceded 1979—and suggests a certain numbness that everything was ending.

For, finally, there was only disillusionment for Zambia as a whole—that the 'peace dividend' for which all the support for the Zimbabwean struggle looked towards never materialised. Zambia remained economically parlous as the new Zimbabwean economy began to grow. Because Kaunda had supported Nkomo's faction, the electorally victorious Mugabe, in naming streets after frontline presidents, accorded Kaunda not a jacaranda-lined boulevard or central city street but a dusty road beside the railway station—through which Zambian exports and imports still had to trudge to and from South African ports.

But Mulaisho, who had been a senior Zambian civil servant, later became a figure within the SADCC (Southern African Development Coordination Conference), formed on 1 April 1980, one month after Zimbabwean independence. The regionally agreed memorandum that formed SADCC was signed in Lusaka on that day. It became the Southern African Development Community in 1992, and remains the primary engine of regional economic cooperation. But, although Mulaisho became famous for his novels, *The Smoke That Thunders* and *The Tongue of the Dumb*, there is a third publication for which he became well known. It was a short paper situated among several that he wrote on regional cooperation in Southern Africa,[49] and was called 'SADCC: A New Approach to Integration'.[50] It was clearly the technical product of someone who would be Governor of the Bank of Zambia from 1992 to 95, speaking about the informal integration of the region through parallel markets of goods and foreign exchange—but it also spoke of a vision. For Mulaisho, the Southern African region he envisioned was a curious writ-large version of the Zambia Kaunda had envisioned. It was of hopes for equality and prosperity, humane economics and human cooperation—and an eventual economic modernity.

[49] https://opendocs.ids.ac.uk/opendocs/bitstream/handle/20.500.12413/7578/IDM%20Botswana%20G%20K%20Kayira%20et%20al.pdf?sequence=1&isAllowed=y

[50] Dominic Mulaisho, 'SADCC: A New Approach to Integration', in World Bank, *The Long-Term Perspective Study of Sub-Saharan Africa*, Washington DC: World Bank Background Papers Vol. 4, 1990, pp. 40–47.

CHAPTER 3

Bankruptcy and Competition

Abstract After a war of liberation and fraught negotiations, Rhodesia became independent as Zimbabwe. But the economic sacrifices Zambians had made to aid the struggle for majority rule were not to be requited. Economic mismanagement and lack of diversification led to a stalled recovery. Discontent grew and, in the wake of the example of the fall of the Berlin Wall and the overthrow of communism, citizens forced multiparty elections and Kaunda was overthrown. With the new free space of choice came a spirit of entrepreneurial endeavour and of feminism.

Keywords Democracy • Multiparty • Liberalism • Market economy • Entrepreneurialism • Feminism

After Zimbabwe became independent—with not a little help from Kaunda's deft chairmanship of the Commonwealth summit in Lusaka—it seemed a huge weight might lift from Zambian shoulders. A very great deal of blame for economic problems had been laid at the door of the Rhodesian rebellion and the subsequent war of liberation. It did not lift. The economy had never diversified under Kaunda's reign and was dependent on volatile global copper prices. Everyday commodities remained in short supply as foreign exchange reserves failed to grow. The lack of incentives for local production was matched by the lack of foreign exchange to

S. Chan, *The Economic Transformation and Political Economy of Zambia*, Palgrave Studies in African and Development Economics, https://doi.org/10.1007/978-3-031-93030-0_3

import manufacturing machinery—and the seeming immediate prosperity of the new Zimbabwean state was galling. Insult seemed added to injury when streets in Harare began being renamed. Mozambican President Samora Machel had a long boulevard named after him. Tanzanian President Nyerere had a key link road in the city centre named after him. Kaunda got a dusty commuter route by the railway station.[1]

Mugabe had won the independence elections of early 1980 decisively—and, indeed, freely and fairly—and his guerrilla movement had operated from Mozambique. Joshua Nkomo's rival guerrilla movement had operated from Zambia, and there was no love lost between Mugabe and Nkomo. Mugabe was disinclined to offer any special favours to Zambia and, indeed, from 1982 to 1987, conducted his infamous *gukurahundi* pogroms against the supposed remnants of Nkomo's forces in the western provinces of Zimbabwe, gratuitously causing many thousands of civilian deaths.[2] A failure to forgive became a noteworthy aspect of the Mugabe character—and since Kaunda had supported Nkomo, relations between Zambia and Zimbabwe never achieved great warmth.

Everyday life in Lusaka saw recurring shortages of cooking oil, sugar, bread and other commodities. In 1985, the Zambian currency was forced to devalue to a fraction of its former worth, heaping further hardships on household accounts and on public services. The huge University Teaching Hospital in Lusaka operated from time to time without water. Public transport began to dwindle as buses were kept running by cannibalising spare parts from other buses in the fleet—until there were no buses left operational. By this time, what had been a white Rhodesian military threat had been transformed into an even greater white South African threat, as Apartheid commandos would raid into Zambia to assassinate ANC leaders in their exile headquarters in Lusaka. This was part of a South African military doctrine known as Total Strategy.[3]

This strategy was launched in 1984 although, even before that in 1982, South African commandos had blown up the entire Zimbabwean airforce

[1] The first section of this chapter draws from the recollections of Stephen Chan who lived in Lusaka for the first half of the 1980s and who also visited Zimbabwe frequently. His was also part of the ANC 'safe house' network, used as refuge when South African commandos raided Lusaka.

[2] Elinor Sisulu, *Gukurahundi in Zimbabwe: A Report on the Disturbances in Matabeleland and the Midlands, 1980–88*, London: Hurst and N.Y.: Columbia University Press, 2007.

[3] Stephen Chan, *Exporting Apartheid: Foreign Policies in Southern Africa 1978–1988*, N.Y.: St. Martins, 1990.

as it sat parked on one runway. Emboldened by that success, a programme was designed to encompass all the majority-ruled countries of the region. Inspired by the French suppression of the Algerian uprising and the writings of the French General Beaufre, it called for different military approaches to each individual country. For Angola, it was support for a rebel movement but also the deployment of South African tank columns. For Mozambique, it was the development and support of a rebel movement noted for its atrocities. For Zambia, it was a slow motion suffocation of resource streams and, as periodic sharp reminders of what could lay in store, commando military raids on ANC locations and personnel. But what this meant for the citizens of Zambia was an increased economic hardship and, in Lusaka at least, the fear of military incursion. To its great credit, the Lusaka population was not cowed. An amazing safe house network sprang up to protect ANC personnel, with a separate safe house network for their children. At the very least, some members at least of the families targeted would be saved. But it meant that the hosts of the ANC members sheltering in their houses were also under threat. If this could be weathered, the economic decline became vexatious—especially allied to a government which seemed bereft of new ideas and new personnel, and in which corruption was visibly increasing. Rumours of coups being plotted began to circulate and, without any legal opposition party, writers began to create new lands in which political programmes could offer alternative worlds, new world impossible in the Zambian reality.

So when it finally came, there was something noisily decorous about the fall of Kaunda. At the Commonwealth Heads of Government Meeting in Harare, Zimbabwe, shortly before the Zambian elections, Kaunda put in a brief appearance but appeared haunted—as if he had a premonition he would lose the elections. Then he returned to Lusaka for the final days of campaigning. All over town, motorists were flashing a one o'clock symbol with their fingers: one hour after midnight; a new time was beginning. But there was very little violence. The polls were conducted by and large in a peaceful and orderly manner. And, just as peacefully but with considerable dignity, Kaunda accepted the results. The television cameras had him ushering the President-elect, Frederick Chiluba, around State House, explaining to him the paintings and curios—and then had him walk out to what had been his presidential limousine; he slowly and carefully detached the presidential pennant and put it in his pocket, presumably as a keepsake, and then was chauffeured off into retirement.[4] It was a spectacle of decorum. He didn't stay 'retired' for long but gradually assumed the mantle of elder statesman and moderation, becoming a Jimmy Carter type figure in the Southern African and wider African regions—mediatory, wise and never seeming to take sides for or against his successors. If there was huge relief that a new era had begun, it was speedily tempered by new tales of corruption and ineptitude under Chiluba. And, to a large extent, figures in Kaunda governments were transformed into figures in the Chiluba government. Continuity was one thing, a lack of depth in experienced high-level personnel was another; but familiarity and, in part, cronyism was a third factor. The cabinet was not a technocratic and modernising one, and as Chiluba began making mistakes, his Movement for Multiparty Democracy began to fragment as a political party—but all the new parties had the same genealogy, all stretching back to Kaunda, all led by men who had at one point in time or another served under Kaunda. No significant changes of policy were debated and it was left, once again, to the novelists to articulate what a new socio-political world should look like.

Cabinet names from the past and who became prominent in the future included Chiluba's Vice President, Levy Mwanawasa, who had briefly been Solicitor-General under Kaunda in 1985. In 1989, back in private practice he successfully defended General Christon Tembo—accused of a coup plot against Kaunda—and made his name as a distinguished and able opponent of Kaunda. He was himself later to become President, as did Michael Sata, Governor of Lusaka under Kaunda. Others in the cabinet included Vernon Mwaanga, Minister of Foreign Affairs under Kaunda from 1973 to 1975, and one of Zambia's ablest diplomats. Even those who had not served directly under Kaunda were well-known members of the top social, economic and political echelons of Kaunda's era. In a small elite society, starting from a narrow circle of university-educated people, and corralled within a one-party state that had begun under conditions of siege from the white south, everyone knew and in one way or another cooperated with everyone else. A clean break from the past was impossible.

What was new was Chiluba himself. A trade union leader as opposed to a former minister, he also cut a sartorial dash quite distinctly different from Kaunda's. It should be said that Kaunda flattered to deceive. His

[4] Stephen Chan was witness to Kaunda's haunted pallor in Harare and shortly afterwards was in Lusaka for the elections and watched the live broadcast of the dignified transition described in the text.

'simple' safari suits in fact came from Simpson's in Piccadilly and his handkerchiefs, which he waved around for rhetorical effect, were from Turbull and Asser in Jermyn Street. But Chiluba dressed like the representative of a Milan fashion house, wearing beautiful suits and, above all, expensive stylish shoes. He had a huge number of these—leading some wits to call him the Imelda Marcos of Zambia—and his constant acquisition of them led them to become the signifier of corruption. Because he was very short, they had stacked heels or height-increasing insoles. Guy Scott remembered Chiluba, who gave him his own first ministerial job, in colourful terms:

> It was in the business of allegedly converting state resources to his personal use, and particularly his purchasing of phenomenal amounts of fancy clothing, that Chiluba ran into public opprobrium and international notoriety. His abuse of the intelligence service to transfer money abroad, and his ludicrous taste in high-heeled crocodile skin shoes with interchangeable Velcro name tags are what most adult Zambians today recollect about him.[5]

But, if Zambia hoped for much and never received it after the independence of Zimbabwe, the release of Mandela in 1990 sparked hope that, finally, change without the constraints of facing down a white south might be possible.

Ironically, Lusaka as a venue, and then Kaunda himself facilitated both the early and the final stages of the demise of Apartheid in South Africa. In 1984, as economic conditions in Zambia began markedly to deteriorate—leading to huge devaluations of the currency in 1985 and a national budget of that year in which 29% of expenditure was devoted to debt servicing[6]—a delegation of two South Africans arrived in Lusaka, ostensibly as Track Two (unofficial) diplomatic actors, but with close links to Track One (official diplomacy), and conducted exploratory talks there with the ANC. The delegation comprised one Afrikaner, noted for his liberalism, H.W. van der Merwe; and another Afrikaner, Piet Muller, who was political editor of the often extremely right-wing newspaper, *Beeld*, and closely connected to the ruling National Party in Apartheid South

[5] Guy Scott, *Adventures in African Politics: A Story in Black & White*, Boulder: Lynne Rienner, 2019: Chapter 5 gives a full account of the Chiluba years.

[6] https://oxfamilibrary.openrepository.com/bitstream/handle/10546/121189/bk-debt-poverty-zambia-010189-en.pdf;jsessionid=D8428E17195F2C6E91DDEFAF14A53BF0?sequence=5

Africa. That the two worked together in meeting the ANC was subsequently acknowledged in public popular media—although recognition through 'splash' treatment took as late as 2014 to materialise.[7] Van der Merwe had met the ANC earlier in London, but only in 1984 did the first meetings in its liberation headquarters of Lusaka occur.[8] Subsequently, both men published their own accounts of their experience in Lusaka, van der Merwe in his autobiography[9] and Muller shortly afterwards in his own newspaper.[10] Kaunda was fully appraised, particularly of van der Merwe's work and potential usefulness, and was highly cooperative behind the scenes. The first night in Lusaka for the two men travelling together featured dinner in Stephen Chan's house—where a rather nervous Muller admitted sheepishly that he had never before dined in non-white company.

This inaugurated a series of such encounters until, finally, the South African Government was talking directly to the ANC—including to Thabo Mbeki in the south of England.[11] But it was in 1989, a year after the military embarrassment of the South African army at the battle of Cuito Cuanavale in Angola,[12] and following the palace coup within the country's National Party that saw F.W. de Klerk ascend to the presidency, that direct talks on the Zambian side of the Victoria Falls took place between Kaunda and de Klerk—Presidents of two countries long opposed to each other. The two always denied reports that Kaunda said to de Klerk that he had to release Nelson Mandela, but Mandela was released in 1990, and this was

[7] https://www.iol.co.za/capetimes/opinion/sas-pathfinding-peacemaker-1696313 30 May 2014.

[8] See Hugh Macmillan, *The Lusaka Years: the African National Congress in Exile in Zambia, 1963–94*, Cape Town: Jacana, 2013.

[9] H.W. van der Merwe, *Peacemaking in South Africa: A Life in Conflict Resolution*, Cape Town: Tafelberg, 2000, Chapter 11.

[10] H.W. van der Merwe, *Peacemaking in South Africa*, p 144.

[11] For the torturous steps see Stephen Chan and Vivienne Jabri (eds.), *Mediation in Southern Africa*, London: Macmillan, 1993.

[12] That battle culminated a long history of South African military intervention and adventurism in the region, always meticulously planned. See Stephen Chan, *Exporting Apartheid: Foreign Policies in Southern Africa 1978–1988*, pp. 57–65. For a note on the Cuban contribution, see Stephen Chan, 'Fidel Castro and the Moment of Change in Africa', in Sabella Abidde and Charity Manyeruke (eds.), *Fidel Castro and Africa's Liberation Struggle*, Lexington: Lexington Books, 2020.

a signal not only for change to begin in South Africa, it was a Rubicon for Zambia. There would be change there too.[13]

Zambia was not a nation insulated from the wider currents of the world. Even with limited television and newspaper coverage in Zambia, the fall of communism—the crowds at the fall of the Berlin Wall in 1989—became symbols that even the most monolithic regimes could be defeated. If television cameras had been present in Kabwe in 1989, as they had been in Berlin and Gdansk, they would have seen an entire city in the streets seeking change, seeking multiparty elections, seeking the standing down of Kaunda. The mass protests were sparked by University of Zambia students in Lusaka storming a shop near campus to liberate bread—the price of which had suddenly risen sharply. What seemed an angry but local street action resonated and protests spread like wildfire across the country. In 1990, Kaunda had to agree to multiparty elections but, as if playing for time to salvage his reputation, said they would be held in 1991. But this gave the opposition time to organise into a surprisingly coherent Movement for Multiparty Democracy (MMD), and it was the MMD that savaged Kaunda at the 1991 elections.[14] Huge discontent over the rising cost of living, despite ten years since Zimbabwe's independence without any peace dividend materialising, meant that the student riots were only the tip of a huge iceberg.[15] The introduction of a dual-exchange rate in 1990, approved by the IMF, also meant that the costs of many imports rose.[16] The efforts of Kaunda to reassert an image of international respect for his efforts at mediation, almost as if to persuade Zambians that they were at risk of rejecting a colossus, included a fruitless effort in January 1991 to mediate the fast-developing crisis between the USA and Saddam's Iraq that led to Gulf War I. It meant images of Kaunda wandering the streets of Baghdad with Saddam, as if the two were the closest of friends;[17]

[13] Stephen Chan was in Lusaka at the time and consulted closely with his former students in both the Ministry of Foreign Affairs and State House where they were senior presidential advisers. Their sense is that Kaunda certainly raised the issue of Mandela's release.

[14] Stephen Chan, *Kaunda and Southern Africa: Image and Reality in Foreign Policy*, London: I.B. Tauris, 1992, pp. 177–192.

[15] John M. Mwanakatwe, *End of Kaunda Era*, Lusaka: Multimedia, 1994, Chapter 12.

[16] http://documents.worldbank.org/curated/en/225961468765047547/pdf/multi0page.pdf

[17] https://www.washingtonpost.com/archive/politics/1991/01/11/western-diplomats-scurry-to-close-baghdad-embassies/c27e032b-b930-4093-9e1b-62d376216639/ 11 January 1991.

and footage of the two men in deep conversation;[18] but the rapid onset of the war in fact gave the impression that he was colourfully ineffectual. To be fair, Zambia had imported most of its crude from Kuwait, but there was no indication that Saddam could break through tensions with the USA and export crude once again to Zambia. New sources of crude had to be found when war in the Gulf intensified—Iran provided the stopgap supplies, but the price of petrol doubled in Zambia (and many other African countries), adding to Kaunda's woes in an election year he had not foreseen.[19]

The 1991 election meant the installation of Chiluba as President, who, as mentioned above, promptly recycled many figures from the Kaunda years in cabinet posts. But this meant few new ideas were propagated by government, despite an obvious early delight that politics did not have to be as cautious as in the days of one-party watchfulness over all political transactions. Chiluba's speeches in his first year of office were full of the joys of democracy and the need for it, not only in Zambia but in Africa and the world as a whole.[20] Despite the rapid fading of this delight, Chiluba secured a second term in 1996. These elections were far from rigged but did feature a number of innovations introduced by Chiluba's MMD (Movement for Multiparty Democracy) Government to reduce the chances of any opposition challenge and which did little to enhance the sense of completely fair processes.[21]

Despite this, the economic situation of the country declined much faster than its electoral probity. As early as 1992, Chiluba made a speech to a diplomatic audience that Zambia was embarking on economic liberalisation and a commitment to a market economy.[22] This process had in fact been earlier signalled by Kaunda himself—almost as an inevitability, as the Zambian economy was not going to right itself under state direction

[18] https://www.youtube.com/watch?v=IDe0_WbQ2Ys

[19] Okechukwu C. Iheduru, *The Political Economy of International Shipping in Developing Countries*, London: Associated University Presses, 1996, pp. 93–6.

[20] Donald Chanda (ed.), *Democracy in Zambia: Key Speeches of President Chiluba 1991/2*, Lusaka: Africa Press Trust, 1992.

[21] Committee for a Clean Campaign, *Presidential and Parliamentary Elections in Zambia, November 18th 1996*, Lusaka: CCC, 1996, pp. 84–92.

Lise Rakner and Lars Svasand, 'The Quality of Electoral Processes: Zambian Elections 1991–2001', *African Social Research*, 55 & 56, 2003, pp. 1–23.

[22] 'Speech by the President of the Republic of Zambia, Mr. Frederick J.T. Chiluba, at the official opening of the Zambia International Trade Fair, Ndola, 4 July 1992', in Donald Chanda (ed.), *Key Speeches of President Chiluba 1991/2*, pp. 49–52.

alone. World Bank data shows that the economy picked up quite dramatically shortly after Chiluba's victory—a mark perhaps of confidence or at least hope in a more liberal government—but plunged even more dramatically just before the 1996 election.[23] Throughout the 1990s, drought and a slump in world prices for copper were significant factors in the decline of the Zambian economy.[24] However, the other factors were very much related to inept management of both public and privatised national agencies, including the para-statals, and the huge growth of corruption.[25] The inequality in economic participation meant that the poor had both no way of uplifting their condition nor any means of economic participation that would have helped generate growth. A whole segment of the population was locked out of economic possibility and economic agency.[26]

Almost as an antidote, the nation turned more and more towards God. Probably the greatest success of the colonial project in Zambia was the embedding of Christianity.[27] Explicit as a reference point in Kaunda's Humanism, it was constitutionally adopted in 1996—Zambia became in absolute legal terms a Christian nation—although this could have quite pragmatic and instrumental, not to mention political, as well as sincere uses.[28] This was completed before the 1996 elections and was a factor in Chiluba's accepting a harsh IMF structural adjustment, which was harsher than even the IMF would have preferred[29]—as Chiluba was confident that a nation that believed in God could weather all storms.[30]

Chiluba himself was of evangelical persuasion, and it was this brand of Christianity that attracted greater numbers of adherents as economic

[23] https://data.worldbank.org/indicator/NY.GDP.MKTP.KD.ZG?locations=ZM

[24] https://thecommonwealth.org/our-member-countries/zambia/economy

[25] Jan Kees van Donge, 'The Plundering of Zambian Resources by Frederick Chiluba and His Friends: A Case Study of the Interaction between National Politics and the International Drive towards Good Governance', *African Affairs*, 108:430, 2009, pp. 69–90.

[26] ageconsearch.umn.edu › bitstream › dsgdp16.pdf

[27] Melvin Simuchimba, 'African Identities: Some Ways in Which Christianity has Positively and Negatively Contributed to their Formation and Development', *Journal of Humanities*, 3, 2000–2001, pp. 12–24.

[28] Austin M. Cheyeka, 'Zambia, a 'Christian nation' in Post Movement for Multiparty Democracy (MMD) Era, 2011–2016', *International Journal of Humanities and Social Sciences*, 6:7, 2016, pp. 159–172.

[29] Neo Simutanyi, 'The Politics of Structural Adjustment in Zambia', *Third World Quarterly*, 17:4, 1996, pp. 825–839.

[30] Isabel Apawo Phiri, 'President Frederick J.T. Chiluba of Zambia: The Christian Nation and Democracy', *The Journal of Religion in Africa*, 33:4, 2003, pp. 401–28.

decline intensified. US evangelical churches came to Zambia, but the phenomenon of homegrown variants was highly visible.[31] In the poorest part of Lusaka, George Compound, there was a proliferation of evangelical churches from the Chiluba days to the present. On one thoroughfare alone, God has now more houses than an oligarch has mansions, each one housing a variant that charismatically claims a true way.

The building of large new churches, even in a slum, reveals a form of entrepreneurialism and cooperative endeavour that has contradictory features. Individual flair and communal effort are not always easy bed fellows. It is a curious Zambian blend, most apparent in its approach to Christianity: the visible becomes a token of what is spiritual, but the communal effort for spiritual achievement allows God to bless the entrepreneur in his or her own business efforts. As the state economy of Kaunda withered away, the ethos of privatisation and private effort grew. As we shall see later, this received 'god's blessing' most fully when global copper prices were high and Zambia attracted high export receipts that resulted in liquidity flowing into the domestic economy, including into the private and entrepreneurial sector. Even so, what began to happen under Chiluba, but flowered under his successors Mwanawasa and, particularly, Sata, was an apprentice culture, but a growing culture all the same, of private economic success through private individual effort. Walking down Lusaka's main thoroughfare, Cairo Road, the kerbside book sellers would feature—as online marketplaces today still feature—used and tattered copies of exhortatory and inspirational books by Dale Carnegie[32] and Napoleon Hill[33]—the paragons of D.I.Y. US capitalist success.

There could be aberrant mixtures of religion and the pursuit of wealth. When arraigned on charges of corruption after his presidency, Chiluba would speak of his wealth as a legitimate blessing from God—to the strongly implied effect that, because he worshipped zealously, the source

[31] Chammah J. Kaunda and Mutale Kaunda, 'Mobilising Religious Assets for Social Transformation: A Theology of Decolonial Reconstruction Perspective on the Ministry of National Guidance and Religious Affairs (MNGRA) in Zambia', *Religions*, 9:176, 2018.

[32] The most famous Dale Carnegie book—and the title has become a figure of everyday speech—is *How to Win Friends and Influence People*, N.Y.: Simon & Schuster, 1936. It has sold 15 million copies, not counting the second-hand copies from the street stalls of Lusaka.

[33] Napoleon Hill, *Think and Grow Rich*, Cleveland: Ralston, 1937. The claim is a sale of 100 million copies.

of his wealth would and should be forgiven him.[34] The charges were never proven in badly mounted court cases, but his image has remained fixed within corruption—even if in the 'legitimate' corruption of a pious believer.

But in his tenure of office other new forces began stirring. One of these was feminism. This, in the spirit of the times, included evangelical or Pentecostal feminism. The appointment of female priests and, indeed, female bishops of new or innovative churches began to be an accepted practice.[35] This did not necessarily mean any feminist knock-on in mainstream politics. The results of the 2001 elections that marked the transition from Chiluba to President Mwanawasa were marked by poor results for female candidates.[36] But new feminist spokespersons did arise in civil society. One of these was Sara Longwe who, as an academic, was the first to indicate how even a transformative election like the one that saw the ouster of Kaunda in 1991 did not necessarily change the condition of women.[37] Even before that election she was developing an activist feminist career,[38] and the legacy of this was the Women's Empowerment Framework published in 1990.

This framework helps planners understand the practical meaning of women's empowerment and equality, and then to evaluate whether a development initiative supports this empowerment. Longwe proposed five levels of equality: welfare, access, 'conscientization', participation and control. Empowerment is required for each of these levels. Welfare concerns basic needs, and access concerns ability to use resources such as credit, land and education. 'Conscientization' is a key element of the framework. It is almost like a feminist version of Kwame Nkrumah's

[34] https://www.independent.co.uk/news/world/africa/shopaholic-ex-president-of-zambia-cleared-of-corruption-1773482.html 18 August 2009. Jan Kees van Donge, 'The Plundering of Zambian Resources by Frederick Chiluba and His Friends: A Case Study of the Interaction between National Politics and the International Drive towards Good Governance', *African Affairs*, 108:430, 2009, pp. 69–90.

[35] Chammah J. Kaunda and Mutale Kaunda, 'Pentecostalism, Female Spirit-Filled Politicians, and Populism in Zambia', *International Review of Mission*, 107:1, 2018, pp. 23–32.

[36] Mutumba M. Bull, 'The Gender Dimension of the 2001 Zambian Elections: Before, During and After', *African Social Research*, 45/46 (and not as its cover mistakenly claims 55/56), 2001, espec. 121–2.

[37] Sara H. Longwe and Roy Clarke, *A gender perspective on the Zambian general election of October 1991*, Lusaka: Zambia Association for Research and Development, 1991.

[38] https://genderlinks.org.za/who-we-are/board-of-directors/sara-longwe/

'consciencism',[39] which was a digressive but deeply influential treatise on equality and the need for Africans to be conscious of themselves as within the realm of equality. In the Longwe iteration, thoughtfulness becomes a key tool against discrimination that creates gender-related problems. Women often contribute to this very discrimination. With participation, women become equal to men in decision-making and, in the process, equalise the balance of power between the genders.

Longwe extended the range of her activism, from suing the Intercontinental Hotel in Lusaka in 1992 (successfully) for refusing to serve her in the bar without a male escort, to criticising development agencies for losing sight of the needs and rights of women—raising in particular the ire of OXFAM who saw her as too radical. But, above all, she was a champion of education for women.

Her publication on the 1991 Zambian elections was co-authored with her husband, Roy Clarke, a colleague at the University of Zambia. The university Kaunda founded in the early days of independence was now producing conspicuous public intellectuals. But Clarke added something else to the mixture, and that was humour and satire.

Satire was never absent from Zambian politics. When Chiluba mounted his electoral challenge to Kaunda, the stately and very tall Kaunda sought to disparage Chiluba's short stature. This led to the mineworkers on the Copperbelt demonstrating on Chiluba's behalf, chanting the refrain: 'Five foot four IN! Six foot four OUT!' But what Clarke introduced was the regularity of published satire in the pages of *The Post*, the newspaper that had been founded to aid the campaign against Kaunda at the beginning of the 1990s. In satirical stories accompanied by the first polished and truly biting political cartoons of Zambian media and political history, contributed by Trevor Ford, Clarke cut a swathe through political pomposity and foolishness. Publishing as Kalaki, after the Zambian habit of emphasising all vowels including inferred or silent vowels, Clarke probably had his greatest effect in the Mwanawasa years,[40] but the rehearsal of political satire between him and Ford began well before that in uproarious conversations in the courtyard bar of the Ridgeway Hotel and across the street in the bar of the Lusaka Theatre Club—the latter also being 'home away

[39] Kwame Nkrumah, *Consciencism: Philosophy and Ideology for De-Colonization*, N.Y.: Monthly Review Press, 1964.

[40] Roy Clarke and Trevor Ford, *The Worst of Kalaki and the Best of Yuss*, Lusaka: Bookworld, 2004.

from home' for exiled South African literary figures such as Lewis Nkosi.[41] The conversations between the three could be scathing of Zambian politics in fully esoteric satire.[42]

So we have a mixed decade of a genuine popular push for democratic change, followed by a decade of increasing corruption and economic hardship—from which emerged a huge entrepreneurial spirit linked, often very positively, and sometimes not, with the vigour and belief of evangelicalism. The two were tied together almost symbiotically.[43] The charismatic inspiring and mobilising quality of this meant a Christian nation unlike what such a descriptor would mean in the West. Indeed, it would be misunderstood in the West as was the Zambian Catholic Archbishop Milingo—recalled in 1983 to seclusion in Rome for becoming too charismatic (and popular) in his services.[44] In a real way, the democracy of multiparty pluralism simply unleashed what had been largely dormant but real in Zambian society under the façade of sobriety in Kaunda's one-party state.

This meant a Lusaka of the 1990s with a dearth of cultural production houses because they had made no money in the years before; there were conspicuous exceptions such as Bookworld and Multimedia—although Multimedia was often subsidised by its authors—but the limited number of publishing houses was replaced by another form of entrepreneurialism, not for the sake of money but for the sake of expression. Self-publishing exploded with a confident vigour and self-belief.

Since there was no hope of defeating even a corrupt MMD at that time, the alternative programmes, all focussing on non-corruption, spoke of a utopia of honesty and uprightness. Curiously, without ever referencing it, and ironically, it was the true apotheosis of Kaunda's Humanism before it too entered the corrupting influences of authoritarianism and the philosopher-king became an autocrat.

[41] Lewis Nkosi, *Home and Exile*, London: Longman, 1965. *Tasks and Masks: Themes and Styles of African Literature*, London: Longman, 1981. Stephen Chan and Ranka Primorac, 'Obituary Tribute: The Exile's Spirit of Bravado - Lewis Nkosi', *The Journal of Commonwealth Literature*, 46:1, 2011, pp. 183–4.

[42] In which, from time to time, Stephen Chan was a participant (at the price often of having to buy the drinks).

[43] Paul Gifford, *African Christianity: Its Public Role*, Bloomington: Indiana University Press, 1998, Chapter 5.

[44] E. Milingo (ed. Mona Macmillan), *The World in Between: Christian healing and the struggle for spiritual survival*, London: Hurst, 1984.

CHAPTER 4

Intersecting World Systems

Abstract The era of multiparty elections resulted in changes of government, but all governments, no matter under what party name, contained senior figures and leaders from the Kaunda era. The shadow of the 'old man' never left. Kaunda outlived two Presidents who died in office. Discontent with a growing Chinese presence became an election issue. The economy became subject to spikes and falls in the international copper market. Finally, in 2016, the elections were won by a party not led by a figure from the Kaunda era, but the new President Edgar Lungu promptly set about an international borrowing spree that would cost the country much in the future. The probity of elections was also becoming an issue. People turned to religion and a multiplicity of Christian churches sprang up.

Keywords Chinese influence and ownership • Political satire • A nation of churches • Death in office

The fall of Kaunda in 1991 was followed by two terms of President Chiluba which were marked by increasing corruption and economic volatility and decline. But it set into motion an era of multiparty politics in which different parties won elections and formed governments, but, from 1991 until 2015, with the advent of the Edgar Lungu government, all the Presidents

S. Chan, *The Economic Transformation and Political Economy of Zambia*, Palgrave Studies in African and Development Economics,
https://doi.org/10.1007/978-3-031-93030-0_4

of whichever party had once served in a Kaunda government. Fundamental policy changes were rare. Personality politics took the place of policy debate, and policy was predicated on the effects of external forces: spikes or falls in world copper prices were the chief determinants of what was possible.[1] From Kaunda onwards, the Zambian economy never diversified. Having said that, within the margins of largely tactical government, uplift was possible—and the symbolic value of governments with apparently less corruption was immense. And, in terms of an external force that came to have direct internal consequences, the Chinese presence in the Zambian economy and in Zambia itself marked election campaigning and government policy. China in its aggressive investing and commercial mode presented a new form of modernity in the Zambian experience.

The timeline of Zambian Presidents after Kaunda is one marked by death in office. All of this while Kaunda himself did not die—although by 2019, when he turned 95, and he was clearly frail, he still insisted on literally dancing into receptions on his walking stick.[2] But those who came after him were not so lucky. Frederick Chiluba himself died in 2011, nine years after leaving office and surviving serious corruption charges. Levy Mwanawasa was President from 2002, won re-election and served until his death in 2008. Rupiah Banda served out the rest of Mwanwasa's second term, having first narrowly won a 'Presidential by-election' in 2008,[3] departing office in 2011 upon defeat by Michael Sata—who died in office in 2014. He was succeeded on an acting basis by his Vice President, Guy Scott, before his ruling Patriotic Front party held a trouble-strewn and controversial selection procedure as to whom should be Sata's long-term successor—Scott declining to advance any candidature of his own on the grounds that a white man, no matter how 'Zambianised', should not govern the country. Edgar Lungu became President, winning the 'Presidential by-election' in 2015, and going on to win a controversial election in 2016.

But the nature of these elections, all paraded as evidence of a democratic Zambia where even opposition parties could defeat incumbent governments, were not always undisputedly free and fair—even if they could

[1] Alastair Fraser & Miles Larmer (eds.), *Zambia, Mining and Neoliberalism: Boom and Bust on the Globalized Copperbelt*, N.Y.: Palgrave Macmillan, 2010.

[2] https://www.youtube.com/watch?v=BP4_RtyOUL4 13 May 2019.

[3] This refers to a Zambian requirement that, should a President not complete his term, his successor must gain an electoral mandate in order to complete the term. The normal five-yearly election cycle is however not disrupted, so it is possible to have national presidential elections in quick succession.

be frequent. In addition to the fact that, until Lungu, every President had served in a Kaunda government, the elections themselves generated reservations on the parts of observers and electoral scholars.

The first multiparty elections of 1991 were generally seen as free and fair and were certainly a breakthrough, ending Kaunda's long reign and defeating his UNIP Party.[4] Having attended the Commonwealth Heads of Government Meeting in Harare just a few days before, clearly feeling troubled and in the shade of Robert Mugabe as the host, and certainly overshadowed by the appearance of Nelson Mandela—milking the admiration of assembled presidents and prime ministers—Kaunda could scarcely contest the findings of the Commonwealth Observer Group that attended the Zambian elections. These were unequivocal in their praise of the elections. The results 'fully reflect the will of the Zambian people ... Our conclusion was that the elections were free and fair.'[5]

However, that did not mean that all electoral processes were perfect. It meant that often imperfect processes led all the same to the correct result and it was the result that reflected the will of the Zambian people. Studying elections from 1991 to 2001, Rakner and Svasand concluded there had been no improvement in electoral processes. 'Administrative weaknesses of the current electoral processes in Zambia provide an important explanatory factor for the persistent weaknesses detected by both local and international observers.' This is to say that even without tampering or political intervention, elections left much to be desired. If intervention is added to the mix, then, as in later elections, many more questions are raised. But Rakner and Svasand made the clear additional point that 'aiming for high-quality elections in countries with limited administrative capacity and poor infrastructure implies huge costs'. Making the administration of elections better than the overall administration of the country is a big task. They indicated a UNDP study that demonstrated that in Tanzania election expenditure was US$8 per capita, whereas expenditure on health was only US$2 per capita. All the same, there seemed a Zambian governmental reluctance to move elections into more streamlined procedures,[6] just as

[4] Stephen Chan with Chanda L.J. Chingambo, 'Democracy in Southern Africa: The 1990 Elections in Zimbabwe and 1991 Elections in Zambia', *The Round Table*, 322, 1992, pp. 183–201.

[5] Commonwealth Observer Group, *Presidential and National Assembly Elections in Zambia, 31 October 1991*, London: Commonwealth Secretariat, 1992, p 21.

[6] Lise Rakner and Lars Svasand, 'The Quality of Electoral Processes: Zambian Elections 1991–2001', *African Social Research*, 45/46, 2000/2001, pp. 18–19.

election observation procedures by international groups did not move forward.[7] It has been as if—'democracy' having been achieved—all and sundry were content with what became familiar, even if familiarity might later breed contempt for the integrity of the now established procedures.

Coming to the 2001 elections, there was the significant added factor that the Zambian economy was declining rapidly. National debt was at US$7.5 billion, rising dramatically from US$6.3 billion the year before. Zambia was dependent on foreign funding for budgetary support and needed at least US$500 million a year of such funding to ensure a form of economic stability—even before any steps to repay debts, the least amount of acceptable repayment being US$200 million a year.[8] For its size economy and population, Zambia was one of the most indebted countries in Africa. Below those macro figures was therefore increasing hardship and economic tension for the majority of the Zambian population.[9] So the question voters might ask was whether democracy had brought any good to their economic well-being. Was it an expensive exercise in an increasingly parlous society?

The 2001 elections were in any case hotly contested and the victory of Levy Mwanawasa was challenged by opposition leader, Anderson Mazoka. Bwalya found a substantial percentage of people polled in his post-election survey were inclined to believe corruption had ensured Mwanawasa's victory, and that the judiciary would not support Mazoka's judicial petition.[10] It meant the beginning of the second decade of Zambia's multiparty democracy was shrouded in, if not disillusionment, scepticism.

Having said that although Mwanawasa and the MMD seemed quite easily and clearly to have won the 2006 elections, what was notable was that the relatively recently formed opposition party, the Patriotic Front (PF), under Michael Sata—with Guy Scott and Wynter Kabimba as

[7] Stephen Chan, 'International election observation is decades out of date. I should know', *African Arguments*, 22 February 2017. https://africanarguments.org/2017/02/22/international-election-observation-is-decades-out-of-date-i-should-know/

[8] Dag Aarnes and Mike Taylor, 'Confidence, Investment and Growth: Economic Developments and the 2001 Elections in Zambia', *African Social* Research, 45/46, 2000/2001, pp. 151–196.

[9] Insofar as discontent might be expressed in linguistic terms, nomenclature for money could be inflected to indicate variations of meaning and dis/satisfaction. See Lutz Marten and Nancy C. Kula, 'Meanings of money: national identity and the semantics of currencies in Zambia and Tanzania', *Journal of African Cultural Studies*, 20:2, 2008, pp. 183–199.

[10] Edgar Bwalya, 'The Zambian Electorate's Views in the Post-Election Period—February 2001 to July 2002', *African Social Research*, 47/48, 2002/2202, pp. 158–175.

lieutenants—had made much headroom in a short time, building coalitions behind the scenes and engaging in a combination of populism and self-advertised technocratic capacity. Voter registration had also improved, notwithstanding earlier comments about electoral processes not improving fast enough, so Sata had a wider electoral audience. But Sata, with the image of enforcer gleaned from his days in the Chiluba government, and nicknamed 'King Cobra', hit upon a particular issue around which he mobilised all other issues of discontent. He focused on the Chinese presence in Zambia and Chinese mismanagement of health and safety in the mines. It was an electoral bombshell—to which we shall return—and, more than anything else, was probably the factor that catapulted the PF forwards.[11]

But, before we contemplate that, it should be noted that this was also the era when satire reached a peak in Zambian political commentary. If Sata was 'King Cobra', Levy Mwanawasa was very unfairly nicknamed the 'Cabbage', not only because he was fat and far from handsome, but because a car accident had purportedly left him for a time in a vegetative state. In the satire of Roy Clarke and Trevor Ford, the 'Kalaki' duo, the earlier single object of attack, Frederick Chiluba as a thieving but over-dressed dandy, was replaced by a jungle of seemingly truer-than-life characters of impossible pomposity and venality. First serialised in *The Post*, the newspaper that erupted as a key force in the campaign to unseat Kaunda, under the canny and sometimes acerbic editorship of Fred M'membe, Kalaki became a household institution.[12]

To be fair, Kalaki never indulged in racist Chinese depictions of pigtails and slanty eyes, but there had developed a certain Zambian preoccupation with stereotypes that depicted the Chinese at least as over-working and, above all, over-demanding of their Zambian employees—not to mention very careless with health and safety in the mining sector. In July 2005, after a labour riot at the Chinese-owned Non-Ferrous Metals Corporation, four Zambian workers were shot. Sata raised the issues of labour relations, management, health and safety, and low wages from Chinese employers to their Zambian work force. He extended the incident to include Chinese ownership of markets and retail outlets. So fierce were his remarks that the Chinese Ambassador, breaking from his country's 'non-interference'

[11] Miles Larmer and Alastair Fraser, 'Of Cabbages and King Cobra: Populist politics and Zambia's 2006 election', *African Affairs*, 106:425, 2007, pp. 611–638.

[12] Roy Clarke and Trevor Ford, *The Worst of Kalaki*, Lusaka; Bookworld, 2004.

doctrine, accused Sata and the PF of being funded by the Taiwanese and threatened to suspend Chinese aid and investment if Sata won. But this only allowed Sata to suggest that China and the MMD were hand-in-glove and that, by extension, Mwanawasa and the MMD were collaborators in poor working conditions under the Chinese and shootings of innocent Zambian workers.[13] It was masterly tactical politics, but ignored the complexities of China-Zambia relationships.

Those did, however, have their greatest visible impact in the mining sector. Having been privatised even in the Kaunda era, ownership changed hands—with Indian concerns such as Vedanta being involved for a period—but with much Chinese ownership from the end of the 1990s and into the 2000s. Labour relations could indeed be the site of severe conflict and misunderstandings. Steve Nakana, however, in his PhD thesis for the University of Geneva, made an instructive and comprehensive analysis of the history of Chinese involvement.[14] He related one particular incident of cultural misunderstanding.

The trade union representing miners sought paid leave for funerals. There seemed to be a lot of funerals. The Chinese employers at first considered it a ruse for additional holidays. Patiently, through many steps in negotiations, the Chinese came to understand that each one of their employees might, as the only salary earner, support up to 30 people. Moreover, the ravages of the HIV pandemic had not yet stopped, and although death certificates as a rule indicated the opportunistic disease that had immediately caused death as opposed to the disease being possible because of inhibition of the immune system caused by HIV, it was clear that HIV meant a widespread early mortality. As the only salary earner, the employee not only was the only one who could pay funeral costs but became a senior figure in the extended family. If he did not both pay the funeral costs and those of the wake, and in person help host both funeral and wake for many mourners, he would lose face. Apparently, it was this last point about losing face that cemented the Chinese agreement to award paid funeral leave. Expressed in mutually appreciated cultural terms,

[13] Miles Larmer and Alastair Fraser, 'Of Cabbages and King Cobra', p 628.

[14] This thesis was examined by Stephen Chan. Steve C. Nakana, *Chinese Capital and African Labour in Zambian Mining 1997–2008*, submitted for the PhD of l'Institut de Hautes Etudes Internationales et du Developpment, Geneva, 2013. Nakana is now a highly respected figure in the South African financial world.

negotiations could lead to agreement. It was a technique, as we shall see, that Guy Scott as Vice President would himself use.

But the funerals example is a case of operational learning curve. In the macro sense, the Chinese might be forgiven that they had gone out of their way to get it right in Zambia. In the early 2000s, the revitalisation of infrastructure such as the hydroelectric plant at Kafue Gorge and the establishment of the Solwezi-based Lumwana Power Project made a discernible difference to end-user consumers of electricity. Moreover, official or officially supported Chinese projects were usually built around joint-ventures, even if as majority shareholders. Qingdao Textiles formed Zambia-China Mulungushi Textiles Joint Venture on a 66/34% ownership ratio with the Zambian Ministry of Defence; China Nonferrous Metal Industries, through its Africa subsidiary, bought 85% of the largely defunct Chambishi copper mine. In short, the Chinese set about revitalisation of near defunct Zambian enterprises and para-statals.[15] In macro and strategic terms much good was done. In operational terms, as noted above, the Chinese could be disastrous in ready apprehension of local needs and norms. But, insofar as this reflected a continental pattern, Zambia was not unique.[16]

Mwanawasa's untimely death meant that his successor, Rupiah Banda, had to face a 'Presidential by-election' in 2008. The Chinese 'problem' had not gone away, but this time Sata did not emphasise it as he had in 2006. Then he had also concentrated on issues such as corruption, on higher taxes on all foreign investors—not just the Chinese—and, above all, appealed to the urban vote—projecting an image of himself as subversive and 'street'. He was not above lampooning Mwanwasa as well by destroying a cabbage in public, pointedly and rudely reminding voters of Mwanawasa's rumoured brain damage after his car accident. Here, the acerbic humour pioneered by Kalaki was used maliciously on the campaign trail. But, by 2008, Mwanawasa had worked hard and successfully to restore his image as an efficacious president—and it was now both Banda

[15] Lucia Ribacchi, *Chinese in Africa: Investors or 'Infestors'? Evidence from the Case Study of Chinese Investments in Zambia*, MSc dissertation, SOAS University of London, 2010. This dissertation was supervised by Stephen Chan.

[16] Stephen Chan (ed.), *The Morality of China in Africa: The Middle Kingdom and the Dark Continent*, London: Zed, 2013. Deborah Brautigam, *The Dragon's Gift: The Real Story of China in Africa*, N.Y.: Oxford University Press, 2009.

and Sata competing as to whom could best uphold and extend his legacy.[17] Banda won in 2008, but Sata understood that his best assets were his populist appeal and his ability to organise support in urban areas. It was in those areas that 'hope' could most easily be mobilised—whether in a meaningful sense or in a delusional manner[18]—but organised, concentrated hope as a critical mass was what was available to Sata as something he could appeal to in his populist rhetoric.

It was also in the cities that the youth vote became increasingly important. Badly affected by the economic downturn, youth, particularly unemployed youth, complained about corruption and ineffectual leadership by out-of-touch politicians. Elias Chipimo, son of his namesake father, a grandee in the Kaunda days, formed a political party and wrote a book on Zambian political history that led to the 2000s with its inability to address the burning issues of the young.[19]

Chipimo's efforts were to no avail in the 2011 elections as Sata at last swept to victory.[20] Having aroused such furore over the Chinese issue, he immediately handed over the 'China problem' to his Vice President, Guy Scott, saying, 'I am somewhat tainted as lacking objectivity in this,' to which Scott replied, 'so you throw the hot potato at me?'[21] Scott is surprising sparing with detail on how he addressed the China-in-Zambia issue in his memoir, despite devoting a chapter to the issue.[22] He does say he made much use of insights from the Chinese African specialist, C.K. Lee.[23] However, it was probably another Chinese female scholar, not credited in his book, who helped most with operationalising Scott's approach to Chinese mine owners and managers. This was Hangwei Li, who won the Prince Albert II of Monaco/United Nations Correspondents Association Global Prize in 2017, being perfectly fluent in both English

[17] Nic Cheeseman and Marja Hinfelaar, 'Parties, platforms, and political mobilization: The Zambian presidential election of 2008', *African Affairs*, 109:434, pp. 51–76.

[18] Ranka Primorac, 'The Modern City and Citizen Efficacy in a Zambian Novel', *Journal of Postcolonial Writing*, 44:1, 2008, pp. 49–60.

[19] Elias C. Chipimo Jr., *Unequal to the Task?*, Lusaka: self-published, 2010.

[20] For a superb rendition of the rise of Sata, with his own roots in the Kaunda years, and his governing agenda, see Sishuwa, *Party Politics and Populism in Zambia: Michael Sata and Political Change 1955–2014*, Melton: James Currey, 2024.

[21] Conversations between Guy Scott and Stephen Chan, Lusaka, 2013.

[22] Guy Scott, *Adventures in Zambian Politics: A Story in Black & White*, Boulder: Lynne Rienner, 2019, Chapter 11.

[23] Ching Kwan Lee, *The Specter of Global China: Politics, Labor and Foreign Investment in Africa*, Chicago: University of Chicago Press, 2017.

and Chinese. Scott summonsed the Chinese mine owners and managers in Zambia to a series of compulsory seminars on Zambian labour law. But it was Hangwei Li who acted as interlocuteur, ensuring the seminars could be conveyed in both legal and idiomatic Chinese to those present.[24] This show of cultural sensitivity enabled Scott to 'solve' the Chinese and Zambian mines problem, sufficiently that there has been no major re-run of what happened in July 2005 with the shooting of Zambian workers.

The brief Sata years coincided with a sudden spike in global copper prices. It meant, even if as a temporary bubble, that prosperity was possible and planning horizons were sufficiently in place for a huge burst in entrepreneurial activity as money flowed in and trickled down. Some of this was temporary mirage, but the Sata years saw a sense of progress as opposed merely to populism.[25] The Guy Scott book is partly the saga of Scott, a white man in post-independence Zambian politics, but it was intended to be primarily the saga of Sata—a protective device to guard in some detail—although rendered in as much humorous detail as possible—the legacy of a very old friend. But the book does not take the reader into the turmoil that followed Sata's sudden death in 2014, and Scott's own brief tenure as Acting President. That power struggle was intense and, at the end of it all, Edgar Lungu emerged as President, winning the 'Presidential by-election' of 2015 and the substantive election of 2016—both against a strong challenge from Hakainde Hichilema, both outcomes disputed, with the 2016 election particularly controversial.[26]

Before 2016 election day, both the Patriotic Front and Hichilema's UPND (United Party for National Development) were conducting polls, suggesting that victory for either was likely to be by not much more than 2%—well within the 5% margin of error and, thus, allowing room for highly plausible manipulation of the results. In the end, Lungu won by 50.35% of the vote (1860, 877 votes to Hichilema's 1,760,347). Two elements of process led to concern. Immediately after the Electoral Commission of Zambia announced the overall result, its website went down. It didn't come back up till a day later and, at that time, there was

[24] Conversations between Stephen Chan and Guy Scott and Hangwei Li. Li went on to read for her PhD at SOAS University of London under Chan.

[25] Alastair Fraser, 'Post-populism in Zambia: Michael Sata's rise, demise and legacy', *International Political Science Review*, 38:4, 2017, pp. 456–472.

[26] For studies of the 2015–16 elections, see Tinenenji Banda, O'Brien Kaaba, Marja Hinfelaar and Muna Ndulo (eds.), *Democracy and Electoral Politics in Zambia*, Leiden: Afrika-Studiecentrum Series Volume 40, 2020.

reasonable congruity between its figures and those of the Parallel Voting Tabulations conducted by party agents and civil society groups at the various polling stations. But suspicion was on whether that had been enough time to massage figures within a modest but decisive envelope of percentages. The website had functioned well up till the critical moment just before releasing detailed data from each station.[27] The second area of concern was the secrecy of the Commission's vote verification. Polling stations and local counts had been open to observers, but as the EU Election Observation Commission observed, 'its observers do not have access to the verification of results at the national results centre, despite formal requests'.[28]

As well as official observer groups such as that from the EU, various governments sent both accredited and unaccredited observers, many armed with sophisticated computer programmes to analyse algorithms and algorithmic shifts. Stephen, because of his local knowledge, observed the elections from two neighbouring constituencies with exactly the same economic conditions, sociologies and voting histories. When one returned results somewhat at variance with the other, and at variance with its own voting history, it suggested that tampering—if it indeed occurred—was crude and rushed and seized individual areas rather than manipulating more subtly across a broad range of areas.[29] None of this proves the election was stolen, although electoral processes may be said to require scrutiny in an electronic age. Hichilema's court challenges were dismissed,[30] or almost farcically not heard.[31] Between challenges, Hichilema was charged with treason for obstructing President Lungu's motorcade.[32] He was

[27] Stephen Chan attended these elections, staying at the same headquarters hotel as various election observer groups and individual observers and journalists.

[28] European Union Election Observation Mission 2016, *Zambia: Preliminary Statement*, issued in Lusaka, 13 August 2016.

[29] See Stephen Chan, 'Free and Fair? Observation of Selected African Elections', *Journal of African Elections*, 18:1, 2019, particularly pp. 13–15.

[30] https://www.businessinsider.com/afp-zambia-court-throws-out-election-result-challenge-2016-9?r=US&IR=T 5 September 2016.

[31] https://www.bloomberg.com/news/articles/2017-08-31/zambian-opposition-leader-determined-to-overturn-vote-outcome 31 August 2017.

[32] https://www.aljazeera.com/news/2017/04/zambian-court-upholds-treason-charges-hichilema-170426133931525.html 26 April 2017. https://www.ft.com/content/de8b6202-348c-11e7-bce4-9023f8c0fd2e 11 May 2017. https://www.economist.com/middle-east-and-africa/2017/06/24/a-zambian-opposition-leader-fights-treason-charges-for-not-stopping-his-car 24 June 2017.

finally released after some months in detention, seemingly after Commonwealth intervention.[33] But it all seemed to inaugurate a new authoritarianism in Zambian politics, some years after the worst days of Kaunda's one-party state.[34]

Underneath this slide into authoritarianism, with yet another looming plunge into economic despair as heavy international borrowing under Lungu looked set to come home to roost after the 2021 elections,[35] without any apology from Lungu for his government's reliance on borrowing as an everyday financial tool,[36] what features mark the Zambia of today? The first is of course the presence of China, even if unrest over shooting of mine workers has gone—not least because 65.8% of Zambian external debt was in 2021 owed to Chinese sources.[37] The second is the advent of electronic communication and processes, including the prospect of electronic voting in future elections.[38] Social media and electronic communication is not as ubiquitous or as well used for political or civil society causes as it is in Zimbabwe,[39] but certainly, if the effort to utilise and manipulate algorithms in elections does take place, then local as well as international electoral observation will have to accommodate new realities. But the use of electronic money transfers has abetted corruption—so that the lament about ill-gotten gains has got to follow complex and often international trails of complex money laundering. The long epigram to Elias Chipimo's book is a quote from Isaiah 32:1–8 in which subjects sought a 'shelter from the storm' under the protection of just rulers. 'No longer will the fool be called noble, nor the scoundrel be highly respected … The scoundrel's methods are wicked, he makes up evil schemes to destroy the poor with lies, even when the plea of the needy is just. But the noble

[33] https://africanarguments.org/2017/09/19/the-real-reasons-zambia-opposition-leader-was-released-from-jail/ 19 September 2017.

[34] Nic Cheeseman, 'Zambia's slide to authoritarianism', *Mail & Guardian*, 16 November 2018 https://mg.co.za/article/2018-11-16-00-zambias-slide-to-authoritarianism/

[35] https://www.themastonline.com/2019/05/04/lungus-spending-borrowing-catching-up-liquidity-problems-are-getting-worse-ac/ 4 May 2019.

[36] https://www.themastonline.com/2018/11/05/well-borrow-without-shame-lungu/ 5 November 2018.

[37] https://www.theguardian.com/global-development/2019/dec/11/china-steps-in-as-zambia-runs-out-of-loan-options 11 December 2019.

[38] https://elections.org.zm/news/e-voting/ 27 October 2017.

[39] Stephen Chan and Julia Gallagher, *Why Mugabe Won: The 2013 Elections in Zimbabwe and Their Aftermath*, Cambridge: Cambridge University Press, 2017, pp. 65–6, 96, 156–7.

man makes noble plans, and by noble deeds he stands.'[40] But this means that both the needy and those with nobility must engage with modernity, both to express need in electoral campaigns and processes, and to trace corruption and correct it.

But, for so many, achieving transition out of being needy seems highly difficult, if not impossible. Part of the condition of being needy becomes a need for external assistance. The turn to God, not simply out of piety, but for assistance in material need, became at this time a highly visible aspect of Zambian life—visible because the need for material assistance was offset by either material provision for God Himself—the building of many new churches through community effort, even in very poor suburbs—or, at the other extreme, a manifestation of self at worship under open-air conditions as the worship of Jesus and his apostles was imagined. The Apostolics in their white robes became a familiar sight in fields near roads throughout Africa, but certainly in Zambia.[41] Pentecostal, evangelical and, above all, charismatic services were held with healing and the speaking in tongues. Whether in a church or an open field, the idea of going forward was by going backwards to the worship described in the New Testament book of Acts—where the presence of the risen Jesus was made manifest to the frightened Apostles by tongues of flame and their own speaking in tongues.[42]

In Zambia, the United Church of Zambia had been for many years, since 1965 at the dawn of the Kaunda era, an ecumenical umbrella organisation for a range of denominations—from staunchly conservative to charismatic.[43] The broad acceptance of worship in many forms underlined a pluralistic sense of Christianity, whether as formalised in European history or as imagined it had been in the fields of Galilee. It was combined with socially progressive features such as the ordination of female bishops and gave an organisational home to the charismatic brand of Catholicism led by Archbishop Milingo after his return from recall to Rome precisely for charismatically departing too far from conservative and formalised

[40] Elias C. Chipimo Jr., *Unequal to the Task?*, p vii.

[41] Thomas G. Kirsch, *Spirits and Letters: Writing and Charisma in African Christianity*, N.Y.: Berghahn, 2008.

[42] Acts 2:3.

[43] Paul Gifford, *African Christianity: Its Public Role*, London: Hurst, 1998, Chapter 5; United Church of Zambia, *The Basis of Union and Constitution of the United Church of Zambia*, Lusaka: United Church of Zambia, 1965.

Catholic liturgy.[44] So when, in 1996, Zambia was declared a Christian nation in constitutional terms, it meant a broad church, but one all the same with key conservative features, e.g. an intolerance of homosexuality, alongside, e.g., feminist or proto-feminist features.[45] But the respectability gained by the United Church in turn 'accredited' the proliferation of evangelical branches of the faith.

It did not necessarily accredit, or even approve, the advent of self-declared 'Apostles', who preached in a style that secured large 'donations' that, in turn, built new churches and a fine lifestyle for the Apostle concerned. Large, stadium-sized turnouts for these Apostles paralleled the similar attraction of visiting American preachers or visits by Zambians to the USA to worship with them[46]—so, whether within the already broad bounds of the United Church or not, popular worship and the popular sense of Christ were features of Zambian life. Certain apostles became noted for their powers, not just of healing but prophecy—and these included prophecies not only of world events but the Zambian political future.[47] Endorsement by a Prophet did a candidate's presidential prospects no harm at all. Even other African Presidents called on Zambian Prophets to help them.[48]

Within this dynamic milieu, with its material manifestations and exchanges, came the idea that God helped the faithful who wished to transcend poverty and who worked to transcend poverty. Hard work towards wealth was something blessed. This meant the advent of congregational networks to aid and abet wealth creation, and this meant in turn a social foundation for individual wealth that, all the same, required afterwards to be shared—not least with the church itself and with its members.

[44] E. Milingo (ed. Mona Macmillan), *The World in between: Christian healing and the Struggle for Spiritual Survival*, London: Hurst, 1984.

[45] When the US Ambassador to Zambia in 2019 made a statement about the harsh sentencing by the courts of gay people, President Lungu demanded, and obtained, his recall to Washington DC, despite risk to significant US foreign aid, particularly in the health sector, on the grounds that homosexuality offended Christian canons in a Christian nation and the Ambassador was speaking out of diplomatic turn and against scripture: https://www. December 2019. bbc.co.uk/news/world-africa-50901537 24 December 2019.

[46] For example, https://www.youtube.com/watch?v=vbAeULc6U6k 11 September 2018.

[47] For example, https://tumfweko.com/2019/03/19/now-prophet-mesala-says-zambia-will-have-a-national-mourning-asks-for-people-to-pray-for-pf-too/ 19 March 2019.

[48] https://www.liberianobserver.com/news/pres-weah-invites-zambian-prophet-to-pray-for-liberia/ 24 October 2019.

The increase in churches and this kind of church practice was highly visible in Sata's brief presidency. This meant that the quest for entrepreneurial success coincided with the spike in copper prices that, briefly, rendered a moment of economic confidence in Zambia[49]—and the inflow of copper receipts, whether it fortified the success of Chinese mines or anything else, nevertheless impacted everyday life in terms of the availability of commodities, the circulation of liquidity and the increase in symbols of material success. It also seemed to vindicate faith in God. Although, by the end of Sata's period in office, copper prices were once again slumping, the window of possibility had seemed to open. Small-scale businesses that, all the same, required a sense of modernity and capacity for international transactions, burgeoned, e.g. the purchasing of second-hand cars from Japan, shipped to Tanzania, and driven from the docks of Dar es Salaam across the border to Zambia, transacting paper work and finance across three countries and two continents, was a business that could be based in a Lusaka suburb like Mutendere—far from wealthy and far from well developed.[50] But Mutendere was integrated with the urban culture of Lusaka and participated in the organisational capacity that only cities provided. In a way, all of Sata's electoral tropes worked for him in his brief tenure of office. Of course, the more successful Sata was, the more God was praised for having provided for His diligent worshippers who saw themselves in the parables of Jesus as the 'faithful and discreet slave' who multiplied the investment of the master.[51]

This had curious but not fully illogical by-products. The peak of such entrepreneurial commitment may be seen in Sata's time, but it had been building since Chiluba's—and Chiluba himself seemed to justify his wealth, no matter how gained, as a blessing from God, as if being pious obviated the need to be regarded in public as honest.[52] God, it seemed, blessed wealth itself. But it was within Chiluba's tenure that Zambia became constitutionally a Christian nation in 1996—Chiluba probably acting under the encouragement of political figures such as Nevers

[49] https://www.reuters.com/article/zambia-mining/update-1-zambias-2011-copper-output-to-top-900000-t-idUKLDE71I02O20110219 19 February 2011.

[50] The authors have friends who accomplished precisely this kind of business success from a base in Mutendere. They cooperated with other such entrepreneurs.

[51] Matthew 24:45.

[52] Isabel Apawo Phiri, 'President Frederick J. T. Chiluba of Zambia: The Christian Nation and Democracy', *Journal of Religion in Africa*, 33:4, 2003, pp. 401–428.

Mumba, a church minister who later became Vice President under Levy Mwanawasa.[53]

As the bubble burst, however, more sinister manifestations began to occur, that tore much social fabric apart. Xenophobic riots, including in such suburbs as Mutendere, expressed violently the sense that competition for scarcer resources was becoming tight once again. Foreigners or suspected foreigners, or simply Zambian residents of whose entrepreneurial success others were jealous, fell victims to mob violence and murders on the grounds that they looked foreign.[54] The dark side of entrepreneurial culture is when the energies for that acquire no resources or capital for investment and are expended in targeted violence instead.

[53] https://www.africa-confidential.com/profile/, https://www.bbc.co.uk/news/world-africa-50901537d/3424/Nevers_Mumba 24 February 2020 for a news-related timeline of his career.

[54] Again, being so attacked and indeed left for dead in xenophobic riots in Mutendere is within the direct experience of people known to the author.

CHAPTER 5

The Political Economy of the Zambian Debt: Context, Restructuring and a Constrained Future

Abstract The freewheeling borrowing by the Lungu government added to Zambia's economic woes. Highly problematic was the issuing of 'Eurobonds' to private international investors, as well as debt owed to China. It meant eventual debt negotiations had to involve different negotiating strategies. These had to be fielded by Lungu's successor, Hakainde Hichilema, and this led to a period of great uncertainty. The IMF introduced special measures that established a precedent for other heavily indebted countries.

Keywords Debt • IMF facility • Eurobond • Infrastructure projects

A recapitulation: We have seen how colonial economic patterns and preferences hugely determined Zambia's independence trajectory. In what were once Northern Rhodesia and Southern Rhodesia, now Zambia and Zimbabwe, the white settlers who came in the wake of Rhodes were attracted by the arable soil of Southern Rhodesia and the mineral resources—particularly copper—of Northern Rhodesia.

Independence with majority rule came to Zambia in 1964 under the leadership of Kenneth Kaunda. However, the white settlers of Southern Rhodesia under Ian Smith declared they would not allow black majority rule for 1000 years and made a unilateral declaration of independence

S. Chan, *The Economic Transformation and Political Economy of Zambia*, Palgrave Studies in African and Development Economics,
https://doi.org/10.1007/978-3-031-93030-0_5

under white rule in 1965, allying what became known simply as Rhodesia with Apartheid South Africa. It meant that Zambia, one years after independence, sought to develop itself under a state of siege. All transport routes for copper exports and all imports, including a vast array of foodstuffs, not to mention petroleum, went through the white south. As liberation movements from that white south, including from South Africa itself, sought refuge and exile in Zambia, the state of siege frequently resembled a state of war.[1] From the beginning, economic development was severely handicapped.

This much is well known. Less known is the Zambian desire for modernity—not just development but modern development. One of Kaunda's priorities immediately after independence was to build a national university. On independence, the country had less than 100 graduates, only 2 of whom had received UK Government scholarships. The others had managed via church scholarships or Non-Aligned Movement scholarships, mostly in India. But that meant Kaunda had to run a country twice the size of Germany with meagre well-educated resources. In the face of a belligerent white south, an airforce had to be built from scratch with no trained fighter pilots or aeronautical engineers. But national needs were paralleled by citizen hunger for modernity. The international press mocked the 'Afronauts' backyard space programme of one enterprising citizen, training would-be astronauts through ingenious but clearly unsuccessful means. But recently, the first breakout Zambian novel, *The Old Drift*, by Namwali Serpell depicted this effort as symbolic of a nation's aspiration not to be mired in backwardness—and certainly not while under siege and attack by white people who had declared themselves superior.[2]

Kaunda wanted to build a welfare state along British lines. He had read Laski and Tawney. He wanted to unite 72 ethnic groups speaking 72 full languages, in addition to an Asian population and his own white citizens. All this cost money. And there was only copper. Later there was also cobalt, but, even then, mostly copper as Zambia sought modernity and development as a mono-economy. It was never enough, especially as world prices were volatile. From the beginning, the country borrowed money.

Zambia became one of Africa's most urbanised countries, resulting in the growth of a lower middle and middle class. But that also meant a

[1] Stephen Chan, *Kaunda and Southern Africa: Image and Reality in Foreign Policy*, London: I.B. Tauris, 1992; Bloomsbury, 2021.

[2] Namwali Serpell, *The Old Drift*, London: Hogarth, 2019.

growing reliance on imports as the agricultural sector never really developed. Urban unrest was countered by the development of a national ideology and a one-party state. People were content, if not fully happy, to endure shortages and volatile living standards for the sake of supporting liberation to the south, knowing the white regimes could choke the transport of goods and also knowing that, despite only occasional clashes, the military had to be maintained on a war footing.[3] But when Zimbabwe finally won independence in 1980, restlessness began to grow. The one-party state exercised control that could verge on, if not the authoritarian, at least the constant monitoring of citizens. And there was still the state mantra that Apartheid continued both to exist and pose a militarised threat. But Nelson Mandela was released in 1990—indeed, ironically after the new South African President de Klerk had come to Zambia to consult Kaunda. The year 1990 saw an explosion of voices demanding a plural party state, inspired also in part by the 1989 fall of communism in Europe but also driven by a weariness with Kaunda and with low living standards. Kaunda had to concede and, in the multiparty elections of 1991, he was swept away from power. But the new era of democracy brought its own significant and growing problems.

Democratically elected governments had to fulfil their election pledges and satisfy popular demand. This was even more the case in Zambia, given the wish to recover from an entire independence era of austerity, and the most genuinely democratic elections in Africa threw up sometimes extravagant pledges of development from the contesting parties. The search for both loans and foreign direct investment intensified and, as liquidity came in, corruption increased. These were key features of the Edgar Lungu Presidency, 2015–2021, when external debt increased dramatically, leaving his successor government under Hakainde Hichilema a huge mountain to climb.

The remainder of this chapter therefore focuses on the task that confronted Hichilema. But by the end of the Kaunda era, at the close of the 1980s, Zambia had external debt of $7 billion, meaning each citizen—with a per capita income of $265—owed $900. In 1987 external debt was 3.4 times the size of GDP. In 1991, the year of Kaunda's defeat and the start of multiparty democracy, debt was 624.8% of total export of goods and services. And 50.3% of export revenue went into just servicing the

[3] Stephen Chan, *Exporting Apartheid: Foreign Policies in Southern Africa 1978–1988*, London: Macmillan, 1990.

debt.[4] Having said that, the debt did remain serviced. There was no default.

So, despite international concern that Zambia would never exit indebtedness, no one contemplated a country in desperate straits. Rather straitened straits perhaps, but no one considered a comprehensive emergency rescue plan was needed. Nor a root and branch structural reform of the inputs to the economy.

Indeed, there were even signs of improved financial management and economic performance—although the latter was always subject to world copper price fluctuations. So that in the years immediately preceding the presidency of Edgar Lungu, there was a form of equilibrium with, in 2012, a debt to GDP ratio of 23.49%. In 2013 it was 24.22%. In 2014, however, in the last year of Michael Sata's presidency, with an 'economic bubble' of very good copper prices and a public drive towards entrepreneurship, risk taking increased and debt to GDP ratio increased dramatically to 49.41%.[5]

In a way, Lungu inherited an ethos of driving rapid development by massive borrowing. But he went at it with a vengeance so that by 2019 debt to GDP ratio stood at 97.38%. In 2020 it was 128.7%, dropping in the last year of his presidency in 2021 to 101.01%.[6]

Indicative, however, of the recklessness that went into the procurement of liquidity is the case of the Zambian issue of what were called Eurobonds. This involves selling redeemable bonds to commercial investors, e.g. wealth funds, with interest payable to these investors. Zambia was not the only country to seek to raise funds, under commercial rates of interest, in this fashion. This had started in the pre-Lungu era. In 2012, under Michael Sata, there was the beginning of Eurobond issues, with a second Eurobond issue in 2014. Under Lungu, in 2015, there was a third Eurobond issue, making a total bond indebtedness of $3 billion, redeemable just after the end of his presidential term. Foreign legations in Zambia were certainly concerned about the Eurobond question, both as a form of borrowing in itself and also in relation to other debt, including to China. On my visits to Lusaka I had several talks on these matters with the UK High Commissioners—always in the privacy of their home

[4] https://www.sciencedirect.com/science/article/pii/S259029112100084X *Social Sciences and Humanities Open*, 4:1, 2021.

[5] https://data.worldbank.org/indicator/GC.DOD.TOTL.GD.ZS?locations=ZM download 10 June 2022.

[6] https://www.statista.com/statistics/457716/national-debt-of-zambia-in-relation-to-gross-domestic-product-gdp/ 23 November 2021.

garden—Fergus Cochrane-Dyet (tenure 2016–2019) and Nicholas Wooley. These were confidential discussions but one general point emerged from my own concern that there was no wherewithal for the Eurobonds to be repaid, and no plan to do so. Without therefore attributing the comment to one or other of them, the tenor of response was 'they're just hoping to get through the election, Stephen, hoping all the infrastructure spending will buy them the election from the voters. They'll delay trying to sort this out till after the election.'

In a way the Lungu government may even have been pleased to have lost the subsequent election, as it left a new government under Hakainde Hichilema to 'sort it out'.

It was default on paying interest associated with the Eurobonds in 2021 that alarmed the international community as a whole and raised the question of how much of the rest of the Zambian debt could be repaid.

But Lungu was determined to spend big, chiefly on infrastructure projects, not all well thought-through or beneficial, to attract electoral support for the 2021 elections. Against this was a civil society not adept at commenting on foreign policy issues, as McDonald Chipenzi has argued.[7] And as Sishuwa Sishuwa has observed, Zambian foreign policy has been a slow pendulum.[8] Nothing has been abrupt after the shock of 1965 Rhodesian unilateral independence—although, as we shall see in the next chapter, President Hichilema has made a decorous and almost slow motion tilt to the West—despite much Chinese good will in terms of restructuring debt owed. But that goodwill and the accompanying negotiations, as we discuss below, were themselves conducted in a tense slow motion, punctuated only towards the end by a sharp rebuke and rethink.

In the newly emerging use of social media as a campaigning tool, as Cynthia Kamwengo has noted, 'debate' could be easily reduced to a rough and ready contemplation of east versus west loyalties—meaning the role of China could be fore-fronted with ease, if not always expertise.[9]

[7] McDonald Chipenzi, 'The role of civil society in Zambia's foreign policy', paper presented to *Emerging Powers in Africa: Regional and national economic linkages in Eastern and Southern Africa*, London: Chatham House, 2022.

[8] Sishuwa Sishuwa, 'Zambia's foreign policy, decision-making, and economic partnerships' paper presented to *Emerging Powers in Africa*, ibid.

[9] Cynthia Kamwengo, 'Social Media Debates on Zambia's Evolving Relations with the West and East: Trends and Implications', *Megatrends Africa Policy Brief*, 21 February 2024, Social Media Debates on Zambia's Evolving Relations with the West and East - Megatrends Afrika (megatrends-afrika.de).

Hichilema, after several failed attempts at the presidency, had built a strong electoral base. For Lungu, in short, the need to stay in power under democratic conditions meant indebtedness both internationally and domestically. What Hichilema inherited after the 2021 elections, and it took his administration some time to calculate the exact totals in what had not been a well-coordinated or annotated spree, was a debt of $31.74 billion as of the end of 2021. Of this the external debt was $17.27 billion. And, of that external debt, $5.78 billion was owed to Chinese institutions.

But the debt was not only to Chinese institutions. There was an almost schizophrenic condition of China and other state, interstate and public institutions, on the one hand, and the private wealth and equity funds that had purchased Eurobonds and expected repayment with interest. Funds like the largest US investment fund, BlackRock, were in no way sentimental about Zambia's history, nor contemplating the pros and cons of Zambia as a future political and diplomatic ally.[10] Its approach was very different from China's and far more ruthless. But Zambia now faced East and West and somewhat different versions of how international capitalism worked.

Even so, the role of China can be, in some Western eyes, almost as a whipping boy. In fact, what the collective of Chinese lending institutions was doing in Zambia was little different to what they do elsewhere in Africa and, indeed, in other counties further afield. The economic difficulties of Sri Lanka in recent times have a Chinese imprint as well. But there are two things to note here: (a) China doesn't force loans upon recipient countries; agency and felt national need are what make approaches for liquidity to the Chinese; (b) increasingly, loans come from Chinese banks; they may or may not be largely state-owned or state-backed banks, but they need to behave like banks with their lending to asset ratios; what is loaned needs to be repaid.[11]

Another element of choice is involved. Many countries prefer construction by the Chinese. The new Kenneth Kaunda International Air terminal in Lusaka could have easily been built by Zambian firms with only the airbridges needing, perhaps, foreign input. But even they are not rocket science. The decision was made for a total Chinese package. Similarly,

[10] At one stage Stephen Chan talked to representatives of BlackRock about the question of state debt. 'Never have I met such hard and unsentimental figures.'

[11] But compare this with older forms of state-based Chinese lending: Stephen Chan, *The Morality of China in Africa: The Middle Kingdom and the Dark Continent*, London: Zed, 2013.

many of Lungu's infrastructural projects went to other foreign suppliers. New traffic overpasses in Lusaka were built by Indian firms, not always to a high standard, when they were easily able to have been built by local engineering companies. Anecdotal accounts claim that an overseas contractor makes 'leakage' or corruption easier. Other such accounts suggest that capability is one thing, but the reliability of Zambian contractors is another. Whatever, foreign debt was incurred and, even with a local contractor, domestic debt may have been incurred. And, in a world of conjectures, my own is simply, without discounting local opinions, Lungu wanted new infrastructure in place as soon as possible in order to secure a second term.

All this brings us to the question of how, Lungu not having secured a second term, the new Hichilema government could deal with the size and nature of the debt. The Eurobond creditors were not development finance creditors but commercial lenders. Their first impulse was not to be 'merciful', wanting their money back or threatening to sell on the debt to vulture funds. The China factor was also extreme, in the sense that an agreement with a coordinating institution in China, i.e. basically the state, can break or relieve the burden of one third of the external debt.

China, by virtue of being owed so much, had a position of seeking to be the primary creditor, favoured in any repayments scheme. It did not want the huge sum owing to be treated on the same percentage repayment level as applied to smaller lenders. The Chinese position and that of the commercial lenders meant that a common framework, first for restructuring and then for repayment, was hard. But the Hichilema government needed the common framework to introduce order and coherent logic to the honouring of its responsibilities. It was undesirable to approach such a large problem in a piecemeal or ad hoc fashion. There was also the need for a breathing space so that the Zambians could get their own negotiating position into order and continue to meet immediate obligations, and that meant a standby IMF facility.

The IMF facility did in fact demand a common framework. From the IMF's own account what was mandated was what was called the G20 Common Framework.

- The IMF team reached a staff-level agreement with the Zambian authorities on a new arrangement under the Extended Credit Facility (ECF) for 2022–2025 to help restore macroeconomic stability and provide the foundation for an inclusive economic recovery.

- The government's ambitious reform programme, supported by the IMF, seeks to restore fiscal and debt sustainability, create fiscal space for much-needed social spending, and strengthen economic governance and transparency.
- To complement the authorities' strong reform programme a comprehensive debt treatment under the G20 Common Framework is needed to restore debt sustainability. The IMF Executive Board's consideration of this agreement is subject to progress on this front.[12]

Private creditors are obliged to join this framework:

> The Common Framework is intended to deal with insolvency and protracted liquidity problems, along with the implementation of an IMF-supported reform program. G20 official creditors—both traditional "Paris Club" creditors, such as France and the United States, and new creditors, such as China and India, which ... overtook the Paris Club as lenders in the last decade—agreed to coordinate to provide debt relief consistent with the debtor's capacity to pay and maintain essential spending needs. The Common Framework requires private creditors to participate on comparable terms to overcome collective action challenges and ensure fair burden.[13]

Non-governmental organisations in the USA applied pressure on some of the commercial lenders to enter a common framework. The BlackRock group was also subjected to such pressure.[14] Even if Blackrock was far from 'sentimental', Zambia's reputation in the Kaunda years, projecting the moral image of an almost lone stand against the discriminatory white south, helped kindle lobbyists on behalf of the economically beleaguered country.

Such pressure, even if possible, would not greatly resonate with the 'new' China. The 'old' China hosted Kaunda in 1974 and claimed that, during their meeting, Kaunda helped Mao formulate the Chinese Three World Theory—a deliberate borrowing against the image of Kaunda as a moral 'philosopher king' at the time, with the inference that the Chinese

[12] https://www.imf.org/en/News/Articles/2021/12/06/pr21359-zambia-imf-staff-reaches-staff-level-agreement-on-ecf Dec 6 2021.

[13] https://blogs.imf.org/2021/12/02/the-g20-common-framework-for-debt-treatments-must-be-stepped-up/ 2 December 2021.

[14] https://www.theguardian.com/world/2022/apr/11/blackrock-urged-to-delay-debt-repayments-from-crisis-torn-zambia

approach to international relations was also moral. But the 'new' China of modern economic practice realised two things: (a) it needed repayment, especially as COVID and US economic pressures helped engender a downturn in the Chinese economy; (b) it had never been part of a common framework of debt renegotiation before and certainly not with such varied partners. In a very real way, it didn't quite know what to do and for some weeks expressed reluctance and even bemusement with the idea of being part of the common framework.[15]

Finally, the compromise way forward was found and China entered the common framework as the co-chair of its main negotiating committee. France balanced the equation as the other co-chair—as the Western 'honest broker', as no debt was owed France. But no substantive talks had been held within this committee as June 2022 began. On the last day of May, President Xi reassured President Hichilema that China was on Zambia's side and looked to a successful and agreeable solution to the debt problem.[16]

But fine diplomatic words are of no substantial avail in what must be hard and detailed technical talks. It looked certain that the Zambian hopes for some agreement on the way forward by the end of June would be dashed and, indeed, talks about talks slowed down as June entered its first week and continued for some time to be slow.

There was a growing international consensus all the same that the talks should achieve agreement—an investor desire to see the talks succeed so Zambia became some kind of regional oasis as Zimbabwe's economic plight worsened and South Africa's economy also performed poorly or with volatility.

During my April 2022 visit to Zambia I was able to speak to several senior diplomatic and banking figures, including those who had retired from leadership roles in the country's public finances and development. They were hopeful of some form of international agreement on the way forward, but at the same time cautioned that there was an elusive sense of cohesion in the Zambian policy machine. Just as the Lungu administration had no central immediately accessible log of who had borrowed how much from whom, so the new Hichilema administration was trying to do

[15] https://www.reuters.com/world/africa/test-case-zambia-exposes-chinas-rookie-status-debt-relief-sources-2022-05-31/

[16] https://diggers.news/local/2022/05/31/xi-jinping-tells-hh-hes-eager-to-address-zambias-debt/ 31 May.

so much so quickly that achievements in one area would not match achievements elsewhere. They pointed out, for instance, that too many teachers and doctors were to be graduated for too few schools and hospitals. Absorptive capacity was not always there. Public administration, in short, could be chaotic even if well-meaning and not corrupt. But there was a bigger picture as well.

For the future, there is no way Zambia can progress, even survive, without borrowing. It has always had to borrow. Controlling, managing the borrowing is all that can be hoped for. Under Hichilema, mining companies marginalised or even expelled from Zambia under Lungu began slowly making a comeback—ostensibly under new rubrics of responsible operation and collaboration with the government. Vedanta[17] and Glencore[18] were among those returning or expressing tangible good will. There was some gesturing towards green energy production, before Zambia and many of its neighbours were crippled by drought and there was often no energy production of any sort at all.[19] Nothing could be enough greatly to diversify the age-old reliance on mining. There are no major signs of beneficiation of raw minerals being planned. And there is certainly no nationwide plan for agriculture under modern agronomic scientific conditions. This means that, by and large, the unpredictability of market prices for metals will continue to haunt Zambia's future. Reducing corruption will help efficiency and reliability of investment but not, in itself, restore or sustain national fortunes. Diversification, agronomy and manufacture are needed. Even with best plans they cannot all come in one Hichilema term. Whether he gets a second term, and I contemplate this in the next chapter, depends on how much pain and austerity is caused by the agreements to restructure and repay debt. At the start of Hichilema's term it seemed there would have to be some very big haircuts among creditors to ameliorate pain and austerity meaningfully. Only China seemed in a position to achieve a significant haircut—but it had no apparent reason to prioritise Zambia for such treatment, and thus set a precedent for others, when its own economy required recovery. The South African Government may have been able to broker some of the debt owed by Zambia to South

[17] https://www.bloomberg.com/news/articles/2022-05-09/zambia-ends-legal-spat-with-vedanta-over-seized-copper-mines#xj4y7vzkg 9 May 2022.

[18] https://www.reuters.com/markets/commodities/exclusive-glencore-helps-zambias-mopani-copper-mines-pay-bills-2022-05-31/

[19] https://www.afrik21.africa/en/drc-zambia-an-agreement-to-manufacture-batteries-for-electric-vehicles/ 9 May 2022.

African institutions, but the total amount here owed was only slightly less than half a billion ($475 million).[20] Without substantial haircuts from several major players or groups of players, the unavoidable pain and austerity ran the risk that democratic elections would oust Hichilema in 2026 in favour of someone who promised to restore some ease to living standards—at the cost of renewed but increased borrowing.

As it slowly and painfully turned out, two major steps were agreed, the second very problematically. The first was that agreement was reached among the public lenders under the aegis of the IMF Common Framework, this setting some kind of precedent for other dangerously indebted countries in the world, and China was party to this agreement—largely to do with deferments and extended periods of repayment, sometimes contingent of a better performing Zambian economy. Cancellation of debt was not a feature. Everyone could say that, at some time, over a period of time, they would be repaid or at least properly serviced over what they had lent.[21]

Zambia then achieved a separate agreement with the private lenders such as BlackRock. But because this was initially on more favourable terms to the private lenders than what had been greed with the public lenders, China in particular immediately objected and the public deal fell into jeopardy.[22]

This caused much international concern, not just for Zambia's sake but for the precedents and indications of future protocols that it set.[23]

Painful renegotiations over another 6 months were required with the private lenders until some distant but recognised congruity could be at least inferred in what public and private settlements had achieved.[24]

All this meant that the negotiations had taken up all of Hichilema's term thus far as President, with default and international concerns being in place in the last days of Lungu—so that the entire process had consumed 4 years.

[20] https://www.afronomicslaw.org/category/african-sovereign-debt-justice-network-afs-djn/forty-fifth-sovereign-debt-news-update 13 May 2022.

[21] Although the Common Framework was not so dextrous that Zambia's use of it could automatically be replicated elsewhere: Brad Setser and Theo Maret, 'Ten Lessons from Zambia's (incomplete) restructuring', *FT Alphaville—Sovereign Bonds*, 12 September 2023.

[22] Zambia's debt restructuring derailed after official creditors reject deal 20 November 2023.

[23] We should all be 'very disappointed' and 'deeply concerned' about Zambia's debt predicament (ft.com) 27 November 2023.

[24] Zambia to exit sovereign default as bondholders back restructuring (ft.com) 28 May 2024.

Lungu and Hichilema were the first real breaks from the Kaunda past. Lungu because he had never served in any Kaunda government. Lungu because the first whiff of electoral 'adjustment' hung over him—albeit within the modesty of a normal margin of error. Lungu because of the recklessness of his borrowing, and Hichilema because of the protracted commitment to negotiations to render the debts able to be handled. It still means Zambia will be in debt for many long years to come. Hichilema because for the first time the problems of Zambia, and the ways to address them became motifs able to be of use to a much wider indebted world. Hichilema because he began some kind of cohabitation between East and West with both China and France acting as co-chairs on the debt issue. But, for Hichilema the first part of his tenure in office was torrid. We shall look more closely at this in the next chapter.

And we shall note that Zambia's southern neighbour, Zimbabwe, can still be problematic—but in a different way to the white regime of Rhodesia. Economic distress in Zimbabwe has meant economic migrant issues in Zambia. Because of Hichilema's efforts to treat East and West even-handedly, without any ideological preconceptions or preconditions, Zimbabwe has tried to curry favour with Russia by indicating itself as 'loyal', whereas Zambia has courted the USA to the extent of a (modest) military cooperation.[25] That cooperation is centred on liaison rather than any active military cooperation. The USA is not militarising Zambia as an ally.[26] Even so, it is even at this level intended as a symbol that, for Zambia, approaches to both East and West are within its foreign policy compass.

And the contrast of Zambia's success in the debt negotiations, even at its most problematic moments, was in stark contrast with the incapacity and lack of foundation for Zimbabwe to attempt similar negotiations with its own huge raft of creditors.[27]

In a succinct manner it can be expressed as Zambia's wanting from the start, as this book has argued, to achieve development within modernity. Its aim was all the same grand: equity within modernity. For Zimbabwe there seems, in high government quarters at least, whose members live in splendour in an atypical suburb of Harare called Borrowdale Brook, an

[25] Ignored by US, Zimbabwe's Mnangagwa flirts with Putin - The Africa Report.com, 18 June 2024.

[26] U.S., Zambian Armies Kick Off Land Forces Summit - U.S. Department of Defense - Defense Department News, 23 April 2024.

[27] Gary Kleiman, 'Zambia and Zimbabwe turnarounds display drastic dichotomy', *Bne Intellinews*, 7 August 2023.

assumption that they should live in a formally designated middle-class society—it seems without the necessary steps to achieve and anchor that.[28] As if it were a right. Dinner parties in Borrowdale Brook are all marble staircases, no book cases (or books) in sight and elongated dining tables that are aquariums—with doubtless not fully happy goldfish. The hard work of Zambia puts that into stark relief.

So Zambia emerged into the second part of 2024 with a concentrated process behind it, which can in itself be counted a success story, but the country as a whole is not yet a success despite the ambitions of President Hakainde Hichilema.

[28] Zimbabwe's middle-class economy ambitions a pipe dream – The Mail & Guardian (mg.co.za) 15 January 2023.

CHAPTER 6

The First Years of Hichilema

Abstract The new President inherited immense problems but he sought to create an international impression of composure and dynamism. He sought to create a new style of relationship with China, while also re-establishing credit-worthiness in the rest of the world.

Keywords Foreign policy • China • Corruption

It is always dangerous and always destined to become outdated swiftly to build conclusions and futures on someone only half-way through his first term as president of a problematic but increasingly emerging country in the world's political economy and sense of strategic location. It is clear, however, that Zambia is at a pivotal moment in its modern history at a time of debt restructuring, huge regional drought and therefore lack of hydroelectricity for industry, and the first signs of paranoia on the part of the government as it realises re-election may well be problematic in terms, at the very least, of not having accomplished as much as it had hoped and promised. Many things, as we have recounted, were beyond its close control. Some things could have been better handled.

The impressive thing about Hakainde Hichilema's first year as Zambian President is how he never lost momentum both in terms of a creatively pragmatic foreign policy and in seeking debt restructuring. However, with

S. Chan, *The Economic Transformation and Political Economy of Zambia*, Palgrave Studies in African and Development Economics, https://doi.org/10.1007/978-3-031-93030-0_6

future debt-repayment austerity lurking on the horizon, his domestic 'messaging' has not been good. Part of this comes down to the complexity of the debt negotiations, part also has to do with his lack of full command of the major indigenous languages. He is a Tonga speaker (from the south of Zambia), and although English is the official language, fluency and indeed idiomatic familiarity with the major languages of Bemba and Nyanja become key for 'messaging'. With 72 different ethnic and linguistic groupings ostensibly and to a critically successful degree united by Kaunda into 'One Zambia One Nation', language politics is still a feature of political and social rivalries.[1]

His predecessor, Edgar Lungu, had consistently harassed and some would say persecuted Hichilema, casting him in the role of a perpetual loser who was destined never to win the presidency with five failed previous efforts—while at the same time embarking upon an ambitious though recklessly financed programme of both prestige and infrastructural projects, relying greatly on foreign liquidity, particularly from China, and also upon commercial borrowings by way of the issue of Eurobonds—upon which his administration defaulted. So that when Hichilema finally did win power, he inherited a country with a heavily indebted economy and a reputation for fiscal unreliability. Debt was one thing. The Zambian affiliation to independence in all things meant Zambia was also in a series of quarrels with international mining corporations such as Vedanta and Glencore, upon whom copper mining depended; Lungu's efforts to 'go it alone' left much to be desired as expertise to replace that provided by the foreign companies was not always there or not always reliable. It meant Hichilema had bridges to rebuild and, as far as possible, relationships to recraft. He has done this to a significant extent, but it has meant that Zambian diplomacy entered the corporate as well as public and economic realms.

But it seemed in particular he would not escape heavy Chinese leverage over the Zambian economy. As we discussed earlier, much importance was spent in seeking some independence in movement and in building a range of alliances to offset dependence on one power alone.

The first thing that should be said is to do with stylistics. By contrast to the bloated Zimbabwean delegation that was very ineffective in its outreach, Hichilema took a very lean delegation to Glasgow's COP 26

[1] Austin Mbozi, *Language Politics in Zambia: Majority* Versus *Minority Languages*, Lusaka: Mulindeti, 2018.

climate conference, 31 October to 12 November 2021, where assiduous work and bridge-building brought a discernible respect for the new man in Zambia. His track record in any case, through successive elections, had been one of advocating green energy and he played this record well. At the Commonwealth summit in Kigali, 20–15 June 2022, Hichilema was again conspicuous by his serious demeanour, and he followed up his courting of the Commonwealth by facilitating an honour for its Secretary-General, Baroness Scotland, who became Headwoman of the Lundwe people of Bweengwa area in Monze on 7 August 2022.

But it was the UN vote against the Russian invasion of Ukraine, 2 March 2022, that saw Zambia break ranks with its neighbours Zimbabwe and South Africa, who had abstained from condemning the invasion; Zambia signed up to the resolution; and this alerted the USA that here, in the heart of Africa, was an unlooked-for but potentially valuable ally. A US Office of Security Cooperation was established in Zambia at the end of April 2022, alarming both the Zimbabwean Government and South Africa's Julius Malema. No tangible military cooperation outside liaison has eventuated. However, it seems to have prompted China to take steps to have Zambia 'onside'. It could not do so militarily, but as so much debt was owed to China, it could do so economically. China saw the prospective pivotal nature of Zambia in the region and, apart from seeking to safeguard as much as possible of its investment there, also sought at least to equal any prospective US foreign policy impact on the country. President Xi conducted a personal phone call with President Hichilema on 31 May 2022, in which he basically promised a sympathetic Chinese approach to Zambia's debt.

An energetic but measured finance minister, Situmbeko Musokotwane, in the meantime had begun serious discussions with the IMF about a debt-relief package. It took some time for the Hichilema government to ascertain the size of the debt built up by Lungu. It turned out to be some $31 billion, well over 115% of GDP. Some $17 billion was external debt, about a third of which was owed to China. The IMF, on conditions of suitable reforms, agreed to apply a formula for debt relief under what was known as a 'Common Framework'—in which all creditors had to express common agreement on the way forward. Many were reluctant but, clearly, if China could be persuaded to come to agreement others would be effectively towed in its wake—even if problematically as recounted in the previous chapter.

The bringing on board of China, from the Zambian perspective, notwithstanding the telephone call between Xi and Hichilema, has not ended and has been assiduously but subtly continued—with criticism to leaven any sense of courtship. Some of that implied criticism was the 2 August 2022 agreement between Zambia and Tanzania at presidential level to refurbish the Tazara rail link, but to use standard gauge tracks for easier vehicle use—basically imputing some of the line's failures to the original Chinese track design. But almost immediately afterwards on 10 August 2022, Hichilema was unveiling the memorial park for the Chinese workers who had died in the construction of Tazara. This was seen as symbolic and meaningful by the Chinese Ambassador. In such ways, Zambia has been both courting China—is grateful to it—but inflecting an independence of stance and action.

The agreement over Tazara with Tanzania spoke also to a regional emphasis in Zambia's external relations and was pointed in its photo opportunities for Hichilema with the female, Islamic president of Tanzania.

China was also given full credit at the opening of the Kafue Gorge Lower Power Station at an August 2022 ceremony (it came on tap in November 2022). Although work began under a much earlier administration, Hichilema shepherded it through its final stages. It means two things: under normal times Zambia becomes 80% clean energy-driven, chiefly through hydro stations like the one at Kafue, and this reinforces his image at COP 26; it means Zambia now has increased power exporting capacity and there are arguments between Zimbabwe and South Africa as to whom will become a primary beneficiary. The Zimbabweans are behind on their payments for existing electricity supplies and the South Africans hope to muscle-in on this failure. Regionally, it all puts Zambia and Hichilema into the driving seat. All of this has been jeopardised by the great drought of 2023–2024, the worst in 25 years, when hydroelectricity simply failed because of overly low levels in the key catchment area of Lake Kariba.

The drought has been the first major offset to an initial positive track record—although no one in the entire Southern African region could be blamed for the drought, engendered by global warming and the 'El Nino' effect on the environment. But, as the initial sense of success—albeit not fully conveyed to the Zambian voting public as prices rose because production dependent on energy fell—Hichilema began to look over his shoulder at rivals and seek scapegoats. By the end of his second year, there were some marked elements of paranoia, and even though actions he took were given full and plausible explanations, the voting public began to whisper that a pattern was emerging.

It was far from always so. At the state funeral for former President Rupiah Banda, 17 March 2022, Hichilema went to great pains to ensure a place for Lungu, with all due courtesies and protocols at presidential level, and the two men seemed to treat each other cordially and with respect.[2]

However, since May 2024, after Lungu announced he would return to politics with the 2026 elections in mind, he has suffered restrictions of movement which he likened to being 'under house arrest'.[3] At the end of May 2024, Lungu's wife, Esther, and their daughter were arrested under charges of fraud and corruption.[4] In October 2024 Hichilema sacked three Constitutional Court judges (the Constitutional Court being the highest judicial authority in Zambia) who had previously ruled in favour of Lungu over Hichilema in previous election controversies.[5]

But the use of corruption charges to harass former office holders has meant the need for an Anti-Corruption Commission. In July 2024 Hichilema effectively fired the entire Commission.[6] The reason given was that the Commission needed renewal, but many on the streets of Lusaka wondered in the debates in bars and coffee houses, in my direct hearing on my 2024 visit, whether the President himself had been at least flirting with corrupt practice. There is no evidence of this, but the mood of confidence in Hichilema shows signs of having turned, and his persecution of Lungu as a presidential rival echoes, at this stage still lightly, Lungu's own treatment of Hichilema. That treatment included imprisonment and treason charges,[7] and it has certainly at time of writing not come to that.

As the great drought of 2024 subsides, water and hydroelectricity returns reliably to Zambia, as the government succeeds in initiating at

[2] Zambia : President Hichilema invites ex- President Lungu to RB's State Funeral (lusakatimes.com) 14 March 2022.

[3] Edgar Lungu: Zambia row over ex-president's house arrest claims - BBC News 23 May 2024.

[4] Esther Lungu: Zambian ex-first lady arrested on fraud charges - BBC News 31 May 2024.

[5] Zambia's President Hakainde Hichilema sacks judges who ruled in favour of Edgar Lungu - BBC News 21 October 2024.

[6] Zambia corruption: President Hichilema fires entire anti-graft board - BBC News 19 July 2024.

[7] Zambia: Opposition leader held in inhumane conditions: Hakainde Hichilema (amnesty.org) 19 June 2017.

least some programmes of benefit to Zambians that are well administered—fulfilling some campaign promises—and as 'messaging' about realistic plans and outlooks for servicing the new debt agreements in parallel with some economic and social uplift for the nation—as these things happen, there may be some uplift for Hichilema ahead of the 2026 elections. But some see signs of desperation and indicators of authoritarianism—even if more subtle than elsewhere—as markers for the foreseeable future. Sishuwa Sishuwa lists areas that he sees as worrying.[8] These include packing the courts. To be fair, many of these areas for worry fall into the realm of 'hard man' politics and are observable around the 'democratic' world. Appointments to the US Supreme Court are political as well as based on judicial merit. And hard ball was certainly not absent from Kaunda's Zambia, despite Kaunda's crafting of an almost saintly image for himself for global consumption.

Hichilema was never given to saintly images. He came to power advertising himself as a successful technocrat. He will be judged on technocratic progress that is tangible to citizens. But he faces many problems of both economic and cultural structures, which will be discussed in the next chapter.

[8] Sishuwa Sishuwa, 'Zambia: The President's five point plan to stay in power at all costs', *African Arguments*, 1 June 2023. Zambia: The president's five-point plan to stay in power at all costs | African Arguments

CHAPTER 7

A Personal Afterword: The Accomplishment and Future of Zambia

Abstract This is a summary list of both strong and weak points in the Zambian experience of independence. Of the positive points, achieved and sustained national unity stands out. Of the negative points, reliance on mining without significant diversification will always leave the economy open to international volatility in mineral prices.

Keywords Unity • Philosophy • Peace • Mono-economy

I have a vexed, at least a volatile, history with Zambia. This said as a caveat at the end of this central section to the book. Can you be objective about a country that has both vexed you and loved you? In which you lived some five years when it was impoverished, and in which you left everything behind to be shared among those who were most impoverished? But to which you have returned some 40 times since? Where at one stage moves were afoot to have you declared persona non grata for taking initiatives outside of ruling Party strictures and oversight but where, more recently, the President has conferred a state honour on you? In this melee of contradictions I now attempt to say why Zambia has achieved importance and to what this book has pointed. As with the body of my writing for this

S. Chan, *The Economic Transformation and Political Economy of Zambia*, Palgrave Studies in African and Development Economics,
https://doi.org/10.1007/978-3-031-93030-0_7

book I have tried to be as objective as possible, but pessimism alongside optimism has been difficult to avoid.

I try to do this under several key headings.

Significant Positives

One: National Unity

A significantly underdeveloped country in terms of social capital—the colonial era had educated only a handful of people to university level, estimates differing from 99 to 120—Zambia was also an assemblage of 72 different ethnicities, speaking 72 distinct languages, not counting those of the Asian and European populations. To galvanise this diversity into a national developmental effort, while confronting white rebellion and racism on its southern borders was a huge undertaking.

The white rebellion in Rhodesia helped in that everyone understood what they were united *against*, but not necessarily what national vision they were united for. The white rebellion certainly did not help in that all the roads and railways Rhodes had built went due south through white territory. In economic terms, the white south could hold to ransom all of Zambia's exports and imports.

But it meant that Kaunda's task on independence was to craft a vision of what the country was for. The 'why' of unity had to be explained in a country where, no matter how many or few languages, literacy was far from universal and communications were rudimentary. How he did this, successfully, was bound up in the following.

Two: Principle in the Face of Racism

Zambia gained independence in 1964. In 1965, its southern neighbour, Rhodesia, made a Unilateral Declaration of Independence—rather than accept British-mandated independence based on majority rule. 'Never in a thousand years' would there be majority rule, trumpeted the leader of what was a rebellion against the Crown, but against which the economically embattled government of Harold Wilson felt powerless militarily to act. But it meant, for Zambia, a white minority government on its doorstep determined to defend its choice by militarised means. And they were much stronger means than the fledgling Zambian state had—with only a rudimentary army and no trained airforce pilots. These shortcomings were put right on a crash-course basis but an expensive basis. Kaunda did not dare risk his new assets in battle, especially with the white Rhodesians able to count upon Apartheid South African reinforcement. Kaunda said that only a united Zambia could resist the threat of the white south, the threat of racism dominating the region. The country had to be armed but, above all, it would use its moral capital.

Three: Pacificism in the Race of Attack

This meant that its fledging airforce was grounded, despite attacks, provocation and taunts from the Rhodesian warplanes. It meant technically Zambian soldiers could not engage Rhodesian commandos that from time to time attacked liberation targets in Lusaka. Throughout, Zambia hosted liberation movements from what are now Zimbabwe, Namibia and South Africa as a mark of solidarity with the core principle of equality in the face of racism and the right to participation in government. Kaunda was very good in his international public relations in this regard and won acclaim for his pacificism—which may have helped temper the extent of white military operations in Zambia.

Four: A Humane If Eclectic Philosophy

With 72 plus ethnicities, languages and consequent thought systems, something super-arching that was sympathetic to them all, unifying and 'familiar', was required. Kaunda declared his 'Humanism' accorded with African traditionalism—although, since his own Bemba people were both feudal and slave-owning, he essentially invented an attractive generalisation in terms of an African communalism. But this was necessary in the face of white economic siege and the necessity of all withstanding it and suffering together. But it allowed an African 'socialism' without taking sides in the larger bipolar world of capitalism versus communism. To this was added an aspiration towards a British welfare state and a Gandhi-ism as a foundation for pacifism. Basically, everything was within a decency, to the extent that, as Zambia slid into a one-party state—unity being said to demand this—even enemies of Kaunda would be 'forgiven' and released from jail after having served a fraction of their terms. No one expected to be executed for treason. That, in any case, would not have been in accordance with the Christological ethos of turning the other cheek.

Five: A Christian Ecumenicalism

If there is one African nation where the missionary outreach was stupendously successful, it was Zambia. It became constitutionally a Christian state. But in a Christian world that was in fact sub-divided into a myriad churches and sects—and where creativity constantly demanded the foundation of more—the Zambian formula of ecumenicalism was in fact a lesson to all. The formation of the United Church of Zambia, where a home was accorded both established and newly founded—often charismatic and syncretic—Christian religion was a step in line with the national ethos of unity, as well as allowing space for radical social reform, e.g. female bishops, particularly in the newer churches. But Zambia, as a nation of God, meant all were, no matter immense diversity, children of an identifiably even if loosely uniform God.

Six: Peacekeeping

The dampening down and restraint of war, very much as an extension of pacificism, has been a feature of Zambian military life and its constant involvement in peacekeeping. This has not always been conspicuous by its coordinated organisation. In the early 1990s, in a malaria zone of Mozambique, mosquito nets arrived days after numerous casualties had been suffered because of the disease. Zambian transport aircraft are not always reliable. The entire national football team, travelling on such aircraft to West Africa, perished in a crash. But whether in Mozambique, Angola, Sierra Leone, Darfur or Rwanda, Zambian soldiers were always present: in Rwanda with great almost *tendresse* to the victims of the genocide—refusing point blank to bury thousands by mass bulldozing into a communal pit, but carrying each body on stretchers, insisting on taking the victims one by one to a burial with a shred of dignity. A Humanism accompanied the extension of pacificism.

Seven: The Return of the Multiparty State

In the name of unity under peril, the one-party state came to Zambia in 1972. It was very paternal, Kaunda subjected himself to elections (without opposition) as a validation of his successful paternalism, but democracy as an exercise in free choice was absent. But, by the 1990s, there was no longer a white Rhodesian threat, Zimbabwe having gained majority rule in 1980 and, with Kaunda's help, South Africa was on the cusp of change with the release of Nelson Mandela—but the economic suffering of Zambians showed no sign of relief. The fall of the Berlin Wall in 1989 was a major sign-post that, everywhere, the era was changing or should change. People, led by the university students, rose up and Kaunda was forced to agree to multiparty elections. These occurred in 1991—where he was clearly defeated and clearly showed great dignity in defeat. What happened in the multiparty years since has been covered in this book but the point to be remarked upon here is that every election since 1991 has been peaceful; there have been changes in government and, even though it has taken time, there have been changes in the genealogy of those who serve and lead in government. Genealogy from Kaunda is no longer a factor. In a country with a small political elite, this has been something. To this, large, extent Zambia has been a model to all of Africa.

The Experience of Negatives

These are experiential negatives. There are few performance indicators for what seem common felt conditions—except for the first of them. These four key negatives were shared with me in a confidential and specially convened focus group of Zambian businesspeople and foreign investors at the Pamodzi Hotel, Lusaka, in 2023.

Eight: The Chronic Mono-economy

It's always been about mining and, notwithstanding some cobalt, it's been mostly about copper. The economy has never diversified to the extent that there could be alternatives or even significant ameliorations to a dependence on copper revenues.[1] This means that Zambia has been a captive of world market prices and their swings and roundabouts. Every new government talks about an emphasis on agriculture, and although there have been commercial exports of vegetables and flowers, the big—largely South African—supermarket chains in Zambia will be stocked as much with South African produce as anything local. Zambia has no fleet of refrigerated transport planes for any upswing in commercial foodstuffs grown and packaged for export.

[1] Jozef Černak, *The Role of Copper in Zambia*, The_Role_of_Copper_in_Zambia.pdf January 2024.

Nine: Public Administration

The pace of development in Zambia was uneven. Building public administration in expectation of multi-sectoral need and regulatory oversight meant that sketchy sectoral development was faced with too much oversight. It remains the case to this day that the civil service has an excellent policing capacity and not much facilitative imagination. Getting new initiatives off the ground can be challenging.

Ten: Seniority Versus Innovation

Part of the problem of public administration and overall leadership is an emphasis on respect for seniority. Although this seems a generalised stereotype, it is a common observation in Zambia. Insofar as it has any currency, it lends towards conservatism, the discouragement of innovation and dynamism—especially as proposed by younger people. A parallel emphasis on centralisation means also long waiting times as areas outside the main cities await responses to their own needs and proposed solutions to local problems.

Eleven: The Unbearable Lightness of the Infrastructure

Although this was essentially what President Lungu sought to address through crash projects and crash borrowing. But transport and, with drought, electricity remain inconstant provisions. The role of China becomes inescapable as a provider of assurance in infrastructure. China is key to power generation in Kafue and Kariba. China is key to the regeneration of the Tazara rail. Zambian capacity to address its own infrastructural development needs remains wanting.

Whoever wins the 2026 Zambian elections will have to address these negatives. But conditions such as the desire to police and regulate rather than facilitate, and the place of seniority rather than youthful daring of imagination seems either like social and cultural constraints, or habits of great caution caused by the years of having to confront, often alone, the white south. They are certainly now ingrained in bureaucratic culture and will take time to dissipate or be ameliorated. The question is whether Zambia has time, and the derivative question is 'how much time?'

CHAPTER 8

Chinese Economic Engagement with Zambia: Loans, Investment and the Future

Hangwei Li

Abstract The Chinese influence in Zambia has been great, and this was accompanied by Chinese perceptions of Zambia in their own media. The penetration of the Zambian economy, but also the readiness to help with the debt issue, albeit with tough negotiations, was covered in the media but always with the dimension of debt owed to Western institutions who were not always doing as much to help as China itself was.

Keywords Economic partnership • Chinese companies • Chinese media • Evolving relationship

Since gaining its independence in 1964, Zambia has maintained diplomatic and economic relations with China. Over the decades, this relationship has evolved significantly, with China emerging as one of Zambia's most important economic partners. In the meantime, Zambia's ties with China, as well as the presence of Chinese companies and nationals in the country, have become highly politicised topics.

In 2005, over 50 Zambians were killed in an accident in an explosion at a Chinese explosives factory in Chambishi at the Copperbelt Province.

The original version of the chapter has been revised. A correction to this chapter can be found at https://doi.org/10.1007/978-3-031-93030-0_11

S. Chan, *The Economic Transformation and Political Economy of Zambia*, Palgrave Studies in African and Development Economics, https://doi.org/10.1007/978-3-031-93030-0_8

This factory is jointly owned by Chinese state-owned companies, the Beijing General Institute for Research and Metallurgy (BGRIMM) and the Non-Ferrous China-Africa (NFCA) Mining Company.[1] This incident brought health and safety issues among Chinese companies in Zambia into the spotlight.

With the growing number of Chinese companies in the country, Zambian NGOs and trade unions have raised concerns about poor working conditions and low wages in Chinese-owned mines and factories.[2] Local workers have also organised protests against these conditions, demanding better treatment and fairer pay. One of the biggest protests happened in 2012: twelve hundred Zambians gathered to protest for better working conditions and higher pay at Collum Coal Mine, located in southern province. During this protest, a Chinese supervisor was killed and another seriously wounded after being hit by a trolley pushed at them by workers.[3]

Zambian politician Michael Sata also further politicised Chinese influence, before his presidency in 2011.[4] During his presidential campaigns, he labelled Chinese investors as 'infestors' and refer Zambia a 'province of China'.[5] His anti-Chinese rhetoric played a crucial role in his electoral success. Sata criticised the low wages at Chinese-owned mines, calling them 'slave wages', and threatening to throw out Chinese investors.[6] While Sata ultimately did not carry out these threats after winning the election, his legacy and anti-Chinese rhetoric sometimes can still be found in today's Zambia. For instance, in 2018, the then president of the Republican Progressive Party (RPP, an opposition party), James Lukuku, staged a one-person protest in Lusaka against Zambia's relationship with China, holding a homemade sign that read: 'China EQUALS Hitler.'[7] In 2020, Sata's nephew, the then Lusaka mayor Miles Sampa, led a crackdown on Chinese companies, including the Bank of China, the state-owned Sinoma Cement Company and private-owned restaurants and barbershops, earning him a lot of praise from Zambian social media.[8]

Apart from criticisms on Chinese companies' operation and nationals' behaviour, another key criticism on Chinese presence in Zambia in recent

[1] Dynamic (2016).
[2] Lee (2018).
[3] Okeowo (2013).
[4] Hess et al. (2015).
[5] Hess et al. (2015), Polus and Li (2023).
[6] Affa'a-Mindzie (2011).
[7] Solomon (2018).
[8] Li (2020).

years is related to Chinese lending practice in Zambia. Due to years of economic mismanagement, particularly inefficient public investment drive, Zambia has been dealing with large fiscal challenges, which were further exacerbated during the COVID-19 pandemic. In November 2020, Zambia became the first African country to default on its Eurobond payments amid the pandemic. China, as the biggest single creditor and a major provider of finance for development, was under international scrutiny for its approach and the transparency of its lending practices to Zambia and the developing world in general. Zambia's debt crisis elicited renewed concern about Chinese 'debt-trap diplomacy' as it is used by some commentators as one of the other examples, along with Sri Lanka and others, demonstrates how China deliberately burdens countries with unsustainable debt to gain strategic leverage. While the term has been quickly discarded by academia, including leading China-Africa scholars such as Deborah Brautigam,[9] it remains popular in the media and political debates.

What is the history and the current status of China-Zambia economic relations? What is China's role in Zambia's debt distress and negotiations, and how does Chinese media cover these issues? What are the other concerns surrounding Chinese economic engagement with Zambia, and how will the relationship evolve? In this chapter, I aim to address these questions and, in particular, offer more nuance to the existing debates on China's economic engagement with Zambia. My analysis is drawn from multiple fieldwork between 2016 and 2023 and extensive interviews with various Chinese and Zambian stakeholders (e.g. government officials, company representatives, bureaucrats, civil society members and employees). The rest of the chapter is organised as follows: first, it reviews the economic relations between China and Zambia; second, it analyses China's role in Zambia's debt distress and how Chinese media outlets have portrayed China's approach to Zambia's debt challenges. The final section concludes with a forward-looking perspective, examining how China-Zambia economic relations might evolve over the next 10 years.

China and Zambia Economic Relations: A Review

China's engagement with Zambia began during the Cold War when China supported Zambia's independence struggle and its post-colonial development through financial and material support. The construction of the

[9] Brautigam (2020).

Tanzania-Zambia Railway (TAZARA) in the 1970s, funded by Mao's China, manifested the deep roots of the China-Africa relations.[10] Since then, economic ties between China and Zambia have gradually deepened and diversified. China has also recognised Zambia's strategic importance in its political and economic relationship with Africa, a country with a stable political climate, rich in copper and other natural resources. In 1997, the Bank of China established its first wholly owned subsidiary in Africa, marking the first Chinese financial institution on the continent.[11] Following the introduction of the 'Going out' strategy in the early 2000s, which encouraged Chinese enterprises to invest abroad, Zambia attracted considerable influx of Chinese capital. In 2007, under the framework of the first Forum on China-Africa Cooperation (FOCAC), and led by the state-owned enterprise (SOE), the China Non-Ferrous Metals Company (CNMC), China set up the Zambia-China Economic and Trade Cooperation Zone (ZCCZ), the first Chinese economic zone in Africa.[12] By the 2010s, China had become one of Zambia's largest foreign investors and a major trading partner.

China's economic engagement with Zambia is multifaceted. Due to China's strong economic presence in the country, misconceptions about Chinese economic engagement with Zambia also arise, often due to confusion between financing, contracting and investment.[13] While Chinese banks have financed many infrastructural and energy projects in Zambia, and Chinese companies have built these projects, it should be clear that these are not 'investments' from the Chinese side, as they lack one key characteristic of 'Foreign Direct Investment': 'control'. It is therefore important for analysts to distinguish clearly between the different forms of economic involvement and do not mix them in the analysis. As pointed out by Thierry Pairault, 'China does not invest in infrastructure in Africa but builds and finances African investments in infrastructure'.[14] In a similar vein, Goodfellow and Huang also argue that 'when it comes to infrastructure, China barely invests at all'.[15] In Zambia, as in many other African countries, Chinese companies—both state-owned and private—have played a key role in building roads, airports and energy projects,

[10] Monson (2009).
[11] Leslie (2016).
[12] Brautigam and Xiaoyang (2011).
[13] Goodfellow and Huang (2021).
[14] Pairault (2018).
[15] Goodfellow and Huang (2021: 659).

often financed through concessional loans from Chinese banks. In the infrastructural sector, Chinese companies primarily focus on engaging in engineering, procurement and construction (EPC) contracts rather than direct investment.

Since 2019, Zambia's economy has suffered from significant debt distress, which has led to a mass exodus of Chinese contracting companies. But before that, fierce competition among Chinese companies for contracts—whether financed by Chinese policy banks or international financial institutions such as the World Bank—had resulted in unhealthy competition. For example, in 2015, Zambian media reported the unhealthy competition between three Chinese state-owned companies for over the US$2 billion for the 750 megawatts Kafue Gorge Lower power station contract, namely Sinohydro, Chinese States Construction Engineering Corporation (CSCEC), China Gezhouba Group Company Limited International (CGGC). The public procurement processes in Zambia in the infrastructure sector to reveal the challenges and gaps therein. Allegedly, Sinohydro submitted the most expensive of the competitive bids (US$1.48 billion) (CITE). When ZESCO selected Sinohydro as the winner, CSCEC appealed to the Zambia Public Procurement Authority, listing 39 reasons why ZESCO had erred in selecting Sinohydro.[16]

Apart from Chinese companies engaging in EPC projects, Chinese firms have also invested in non-ferrous mining, manufacturing, agriculture, among other sectors. According to data from the Chinese Ministry of Commerce, the stock of Chinese direct investment in Zambia reached US$3.055 billion by the end of 2020.[17] While there is no official figure on the number of Chinese companies operating in Zambia, existing studies have found that the number is fairly large. A 2017 survey estimated that the number of Chinese companies (including small-size enterprises) in Zambia was close to 900. Aside from Nigeria, this is the largest number on the continent.[18] Additionally, according to a Chinese community leader's estimate, there were over 1000 Chinese companies operating in Zambia by 2020,[19] despite some companies left due to the pandemic and Zambia's debt distress.

[16] Interviews with senior managers from ZESCO, Lusaka, April and May 2016.
[17] Chinese Academy of International Trade and Economic Cooperation et al. (2020).
[18] Sun et al. (2017).
[19] Che (2020).

Chinese investments have undeniably contributed to Zambia's much-needed economic growth and yielded significant benefits, such as job creation, human capital development and certain level of technology transfer. However, these investments have also sparked concerns regarding labour law violations, environmental impacts—particularly related to mukula (rosewood) trade,[20] corruption, limited spillover effects[21] and other complex issues. Of course, such criticism should not be directed at Chinese companies alone, as the popular saying goes, 'it takes two to tangle'. On corruption, for instance, a Chinese entrepreneur in Zambia shared with me: 'In an ideal world, there is no corruption. We don't like bribing government officials. But in Zambia, if you want to get things done, you have to pay extra money. It's not that we want to pay the officials; often, it's the officials, officers, and police who ask us for money. If we don't give them what they ask for, we are in trouble.'[22]

The Zambian government, particularly relevant regulatory bodies, is not necessarily passive when it comes to regulating foreign companies' operation and guaranteeing local workers' safety.[23] However, challenges within many bureaucratic organisations, such as a lack of staff and inadequate funding, make enforcement, regulation and implementation of certain policies difficult. For instance, according to the Minister of Labour Joyce Nonde (Lungu's term), in 2019, the Ministry of Labour 'had 110 inspectors, there should be at least 1000 to fulfil its monitoring functions ... We are caught up by the situation and we don't know what to do.'[24]

Zambia's Debt Crisis and Chinese Media Discourse

As mentioned, key criticism on Chinese engagement with Zambia in recent years is about debt. But, first what exactly is China's role in Zambia's debt distress? Scholars calculated that 18 major and minor Chinese financiers have provided external loans to Zambia and its SOEs since 2000. Additionally, loan commitments by Chinese financiers between 2000 and 2020 totalled $10.3 billion, with 67% ($6.94 billion) committed just since

[20] Cerutti et al. (2022).

[21] Kopiński et al. (2023), Li et al. (2022).

[22] Interview with a Chinese entrepreneur in Zambia, Lusaka, 5 August 2023.

[23] Dynamic (2016).

[24] Interview with Joyce Nonde-Simukoko, the then Minister of Labour, Lusaka, 07.05. 2019.

2015.[25] Many of the Chinese loans were also accumulated during Edgar Lungu's presidency (January 2015 to August 2021). As repeatedly pointed by interviewees during my fieldwork, Lungu and his team planned to use Chinese-financed projects as campaign capital, showcasing his commitments to improving the country's infrastructure and citizens' life.[26] Meanwhile, through corruption, he could further accumulate capital from various Chinese companies, who often fought fiercely over the same contracts and were willing to pay high amount of 'lobbying fee' or commission fee to politicians.

While China is the single biggest creditor, Zambia has also borrowed from others, including the development banks and the commercial Eurobond market. China, along with other creditors, has been involved in extensive discussions on how to restructure the country's debt. China has also participated in debt-relief efforts under the G20's Common Framework for Debt Treatments. However, negotiations have been complex, due to the many Chinese actors involved. Apart from China's two major policy banks, the China Development Bank (CDB) and the Export-Import Bank of China (Exim), other commercial banks, such as the Industrial and Commercial Bank of China (ICBC), the Bank of China, Jiangxi Bank Co., Ltd., as well as various contractors (e.g. Sinohydro, ZTE), were also the lenders to Zambia.[27] As of June 2023, Zambia finally achieved a significant milestone by securing a loan restructuring agreement worth $6.3 billon, including $4.1 billion owed to China. The 2023 debt restructuring agreement was a result of collaborative efforts under the G20 Common Framework, with China co-chairing the creditor committee.

While we are familiar with how international media have reported on Zambia's debt distress, we know less about how Chinese media outlets have covered the issue and portrayed China's approach to Zambia's debt challenges. Over the past years, Chinese media (Xinhua, *China Daily, People's Daily, and Global Times*) have also been proactive in addressing and refuting criticisms that Chinese lending practices are exploitative or designed to trap other Global South countries in a cycle of debt. Many

[25] Brautigam and Wang (2021).

[26] Multiple interviews with Zambian officials and managers of various Chinese companies, Lusaka, 2016, 2017, 2019.

[27] More details about the Chinese lenders and Zambian debt, please see the database from Boston University's Global Development Policy Center: https://www.bu.edu/gdp/chinese-loans-to-africa-database/

Chinese media outlets have pushed back against the 'debt-trap diplomacy' narrative.[28] In the Zambian context, Chinese media coverage highlight that a significant portion of Zambia's debt is owed to bondholders and multilateral institutions, rather than to China, arguing bondholders and Western institutions should take greater responsibility for addressing Zambia's debt burden. Such argument is closely align with that of the Chinese government. As Chinese government spokespersons claimed, 'commercial creditors and multilateral financial institutions, which are predominantly Western, account for 70 per cent of Zambia's external debt, and it is only right that they should shoulder their responsibilities and act more vigorously to alleviate Zambia's debt burden.'[29]

Meanwhile, Chinese media also highlight China's 'constructive'[30] role in facilitating debt relief and economic recovery, including participation in the G20 Common Framework and bilateral debt suspension agreements, portraying China as a responsible creditor. For example, in an article titled 'Chinese assistance holds key for Zambia',[31] *China Daily* praised China's proactive role in restructuring debts in Zambia. In a similar vein, Xinhua has reported extensively on China's willingness to engage in debt restructuring talks, citing the country's active participation in the G20 Debt Service Suspension Initiative (DSSI), framing these efforts as evidence of China's commitment to global financial stability and its role as a constructive player in international finance. This framing seeks to portray China as a contributor to global debt-relief efforts rather than a contributor to Zambia's financial distress.

Moreover, Chinese media have also avoided directly confronting the criticism that Zambia's debt crisis is partly due to overly ambitious and poorly managed projects funded by Chinese loans. And compared to the more concerning tone surrounding Zambia's economic development in international media outlets, Chinese media presented it in a much more optimistic light. For instance, Xinhua published an article on the optimistic attitude among Zambian business community about Zambia's debt deal, which will lead to increased investment and economic growth in the country.[32] Chinese media have also avoided directly confronting the

[28] For instance, see: Wang and Zhao (2024).
[29] Wang and Zhang (2023).
[30] *Pengpai* (2023).
[31] Mulenga (2024).
[32] Xinhua (2024).

criticism that Zambia's debt crisis is partly due to overly ambitious and poorly managed projects funded by Chinese loans. Corruption scandals that are associated with Chinese loans are also not covered.

The reality of Zambia's debt challenges underscores the need for greater transparency and coordination in China's lending practices, which have not been openly discussed among Chinese media or Chinese intellectuals. While it is not openly covered, these issues were internally discussed among Chinese policymakers, SOE managers and academics through internal workshops or internal references. For instance, the unhealthy competition among Chinese contractors, despite difficult to address, is a topic frequently discussed among Chinese policymakers.[33] Improving better coordination in China's international development is also another topic that has been frequently discussed.[34]

How Will the Zambia-China Relations Evolve?

With the launch of China's Belt and Road Initiative in 2013, China prioritised infrastructure projects for several years, especially roads, airports and railways. Due to China's domestic economic challenges, particularly its domestic debt, Chinese lending to Africa has become more cautious and moderate in recent years (especially since the pandemic). It is, of course, also a learning experience for China, especially its policy banks, in terms of how to lend more responsibly, after receiving significant pushback from host countries' media, civil society and opposition parties regarding its lending practices in Africa.[35] Zambia's debt risks also remind China the risks associated with large-scale borrowing. As observed by scholars and commentators, China has been adjusting the types and sectors of the projects it funds.[36] More recently, and at least partly in response to growing criticism of the BRI, China has been promoting the so-called small yet beautiful[37] approach: smaller and more targeted projects that are both economically viable and make a positive contribution to the environment and social development.[38]

[33] Multiple interviews with Chinese policymakers and academics, Beijing, 2022 and 2023.
[34] Ibid.
[35] Li and Wang (2023).
[36] Ray (2023), Li and Hackenesch (2024).
[37] Ray (2023).
[38] Li and Hackenesch (2024).

This trend is somehow also evident in Zambia. According to Boston University's Global Development Policy Center's database, from 2020 to 2024, China has only financed two road projects in Zambia,[39] a sharp decline compared to previous years. While it is predictable Chinese financing in Zambia will be much less, the revitalisation of the TAZARA railway is on China's agenda. For China, the legacy of the TAZARA railway makes it an important and eloquent manifestation of South-South Cooperation during very difficult times. As such, it has become both political and historical symbol for China, extending beyond its economic significance. Thus, China has proposed in February 2024 to invest US$1 billion to revitalise the railway. During the latest FOCAC in September 2024, Chinese President Xi, Tanzanian President Hassan and Zambian President Hichilema witnessed the signing of MoU on revitalising the TAZARA railway.[40]

Moreover, Chinese companies, especially private investors, also demonstrate resilience and also steep learning curves. As Lee claimed that 'outbound Chinese investors have had to climb a steep learning curve in dealing with types of politics not found in their own country'.[41] As observed by Lee, in Zambia, Chinese companies have had to navigate challenges such as resource nationalism, adversarial trade unions and moral criticism of their work culture. These pressures from African states and local workers' interests have forced Chinese businesses to adjust and compromise their practices.[42] Many of these companies, in contrast to the typically project-based construction firms, are actively seeking ways to establish a lasting presence and achieve long-term success in Zambia.

On the Zambian side, local actors have also gained more experience in working with Chinese counterparts. They have the potential to play a greater role in monitoring labour practices, facilitating local content, and enforcing environmental regulations, ensuring that Zambians gain meaningful benefits from foreign investment and that Chinese investments adequately benefit the citizens of Zambia. For instance, in 2019, when I spoke to many of my Chinese interviewees, they had never even heard of the Zambia Development Agency (ZDA), which is responsible for monitoring the spillover effects of foreign companies. However, in 2023, when

[39] The data is available here: https://www.bu.edu/gdp/chinese-loans-to-africa-database/

[40] Liu (2024).

[41] Lee (2018).

[42] Ibid.

I returned to Zambia, I saw that ZDA had collaborated much more with Chinese associations, organising events and activities to promote stronger linkages between Chinese firms and local companies. In February 2025, the Zambia Institute for Policy Analysis and Research (ZIPAR), a think tank established by the Government of Zambia, hosted a workshop to explore the dynamics of Chinese investments in Zambia and strategies to maximise local benefits—an area that can be further explored between Zambian NGOs, civil society and Chinese companies, which have become more interested and involved in corporate social responsibility (CSR).

Last but not least, the debt challenges in Zambia offer a crucial lesson for the Zambian government regarding loans. According to the 2016 Constitution, the government is required to seek parliamentary approval for borrowing; yet, this has often been overlooked. There have also been repeated calls for greater transparency in the loan contracting process, whether from China or elsewhere. A more inclusive approach that involves greater consultation with the national assembly and more actors (e.g. civil society, academics, NGOs), and not just the executive arm of government, is needed.[43]

Bibliography

Affa'a-Mindzie, M. (2011). Zambia's Presidential Election: A Referendum on China's Investment. *IPI*. Available at: https://theglobalobservatory.org/2011/10/zambias-presidential-election-a-referendum-on-chinas-investment/

Brautigam, D. (2020). A critical look at Chinese 'debt-trap diplomacy': The rise of a meme. *Area Development and Policy, 5*(1), 1–14.

Brautigam, D., & Wang, Y. (2021). Zambia's Chinese debt in the pandemic era (No. 05/2021). *Briefing Paper*.

Brautigam, D., & Xiaoyang, T. (2011). African Shenzhen: China's special economic zones in Africa. *The Journal of Modern African Studies, 49*(1), 27–54.

Brautigam, D. (2021). How Zambia and China Co-Created a Debt "Tragedy of the Commons" (No. 2021/51). *Working Paper*.

Cerutti, P. O., Gumbo, D., Moombe, K., Schoneveld, G., Nasi, R., Bourland, N., & Weng, X. (2022). Informality, global capital, rural development and the environment: Mukula (rosewood) trade between China and Zambia.

[43] Hampwaye et al. (2023, p. 179).

Che, J. (2020). Zanbiya huaren shehui saomiao [Scan of Chinese community in Zambia], *Qiaowang*, 4 September. http://www.qiaowang.org/m/view.php?aid=13693

Chinese Academy of International Trade and Economic Cooperation, Economic and Commercial Section of the Embassy of the People's Republic of China in Zambia, Ministry of Commerce of the People's Republic of China. (2020). Guide to Foreign Investment and Cooperation Countries (Regions): Zambia. https://fdi.mofcom.gov.cn/resource/pdf/2022/04/07/ff4eddc473d246b1a53945a7aa8a406b.pdf

Dynamic, B. (2016). Fighting the race to the bottom: Regulating Chinese investment in Zambian mines. *Made in China Journal*. Available at: https://madeinchinajournal.com/2016/09/27/fighting-the-race-to-the-bottom-regulating-chinese-investment-in-zambian-mines/

Goodfellow, T., & Huang, Z. (2021). Contingent infrastructure and the dilution of 'Chineseness'. *Environment and Planning: Economy and Space, 53*(4), 655–674.

Hampwaye, G., Carmody, P., & Ramaloko, P. M. (2023). China-Zambia engagements: Is there change, what has changed, and why? *Journal of Contemporary East Asia Studies, 12*(1), 179–198.

Hess, S., Aidoo, R., Hess, S., & Aidoo, R. (2015). King Cobra and the Rise of Anti-Chinese Populism in Zambia. *Charting the Roots of Anti-Chinese Populism in Africa*, 25–39.

Kopiński, D., Carmody, P., & Taylor, I. (2023). *The political economy of Chinese FDI and spillover effects in Africa*. Springer Nature.

Lee, C. K. (2018). *The specter of global China: Politics, labor, and foreign investment in Africa*. University of Chicago Press.

Leslie, A. N. (2016). Zambia and China: Workers' protest, civil society, and the role of opposition politics in elevating state engagement. *African Studies Quarterly, 16*(3 & 4), 89–106.

Li, H. (2020). China and Africa: The "Other" in the time of pandemic. *Italian Institute for International Political Studies*. Available at: https://www.ispionline.it/en/pubblicazione/china-and-africa-other-time-pandemic-26461

Li, H. (2023). Chinese investors in Zambia and Angola: Motives, profile, strategies. In *The Political Economy of Chinese FDI and Spillover Effects in Africa* (pp. 193–216). Cham: Springer International Publishing.

Li, H., & Shi, X. (2019). Home away from home: The social and political roles of contemporary Chinese associations in Zambia. *Journal of Current Chinese Affairs, 48*(2), 148–170.

Li, H., Kopiński, D., & Taylor, I. (2022). China and the troubled prospects for Africa's economic take-off: Linkage formation and spillover effects in Zambia. *Journal of Southern African Studies, 48*(5), 861–882.

Li, H., & Wang, Y. (2023). African media cultures and Chinese public relations strategies in Kenya and Ethiopia. *Carnegie Endowment for International Peace.*

Li, H., & Hackenesch, C. (2024). FOCAC 2024: Moving away from large infrastructure deals towards normative power of China. *Megatrends Afrika Spotlight, 16* September. www.megatrends-afrika.de/en/publication/megatrends-spotlight-38-focac-2024-towards-normative-power-of-china.

Liu, X. (2024). MoU signed to revitalize TAZARA railway. *Global Times.* Available at: https://www.globaltimes.cn/page/202409/1319255.shtml

Monson, J. (2009). *Africa's Freedom Railway: How a Chinese development project changed lives and livelihoods in Tanzania.* Indiana University Press.

Mulenga, Chali. (2024). Chinese assistance holds key for Zambia. *China Daily.* Available at: https://www.chinadaily.com.cn/a/202406/20/WS66739166a31095c51c509e34.html

Polus, A., & Li, H. (2023). Development studies meet Pierre Bourdieu: The case of Chinese private FDI in Zambia. *The Journal of Modern African Studies, 61*(4), 521–543.

Pairault, T. (2018). China in Africa: Goods supplier, service provider rather than investor. *Bridges Africa, 7*(5), 17–22.

Ray, R. (2023). 'Small is beautiful': A new era in China's overseas development finance? *Global China Initiative Policy Brief, 17*, 19.

Solomon, S. (2018). Zambia's sovereignty concerns put China in crosshairs. *VOA.* Available at: https://www.voanews.com/a/zambia-sovereignty-concerns-put-china-in-crosshairs/4586797.html

Sun, I. Y., Jayaram, K. & Kassiri, O. (2017). Dance of the lions and dragons: how are Africa and China engaging, and how will the partnership evolve? Mckinsey Report. Available at: https://www.mckinsey.com/~/media/mckinsey/featured%20insights/middle%20east%20and%20africa/the%20closest%20look%20yet%20at%20chinese%20economic%20engagement%20in%20africa/dance-of-the-lions-and-dragons.ashx

Wang, L., & Zhang, W. (2023). 外交部:中方将继续为赞比亚债务问题的解决发挥建设性作用 [Foreign Ministry: China will continue to play constructive role in resolving Zambia's debt problem]. *Pengpai.* https://www.thepaper.cn/newsDetail_forward_22093693

Wang, Z., & Zhao, Z. (2024). (FOCAC) Explainer: Why Africans won't buy the "Debt Trap" narrative against China. *Xinhua.* Available at: https://english.news.cn/20240901/5211979c6a534b3daff274425a9329c8/c.html

Xinhua. (2024). Zambian business community optimistic about debt deal for investment boost. Available at: https://english.news.cn/africa/20240329/52f00a21de3b4532a556a585312d53a9/c.html

CHAPTER 9

'It Will All End in Tears': The Politics of Debt and the Spread of Misinformation on Zambian Social Media

Cynthia M. Kamwengo

Abstract Over the last decade, Zambian social media has been dominated by debates about foreign influence over the economy, the embezzlement of public funds, and the country's descent into a debt crisis. The current government led by the United Party for National Development (UPND) has often used social media to share updates about its complex negotiations for debt treatment and its plans for economic reconstruction involving bilateral partners, multilateral organisations and private financial institutions. Opposition political parties tend to offer counternarratives that critique the UPND's reliance on external assistance, including what appears to be the International Monetary Fund's (IMF) central function and the Chinese government's diminished position. They also argue that the Zambian public will cry at the end of the UPND's tenure when they realise that the government has mismanaged the process and further damaged the economy. This chapter examines social media narratives about Zambia's debt and demonstrates how social media platforms have emerged as key spaces for public debate, tools for spreading political misinformation, as well as digital archives of Zambia's twenty-first-century political history.

The original version of the chapter has been revised. A correction to this chapter can be found at https://doi.org/10.1007/978-3-031-93030-0_11

S. Chan, *The Economic Transformation and Political Economy of Zambia*, Palgrave Studies in African and Development Economics, https://doi.org/10.1007/978-3-031-93030-0_9

Keywords Social media • Misinformation • IMF • Debt treatment

Introduction

Zambia's debt burden and the government's relationship with the country's foreign creditors have historically been a source of intense public debate. The most significant debates took place during the 1990s, when revenues generated by the copper industry were low and the government's dependence on external financial assistance was high. It attempted to stabilise the economy through policy reforms that were part of the Structural Adjustment Programme (SAP) that the International Monetary Fund (IMF) and World Bank mandated as a condition for their financial assistance. However, its imposition of a freeze on public sector wages and privatisation of state-owned enterprises (SOEs) resulted in a sudden rise in the rate of unemployment and a massive brain drain as highly skilled workers moved abroad to obtain better opportunities. Cuts to public spending on education, healthcare and social safety nets further contributed to a deterioration in the living standards of the average Zambian household.[1] A complex number of issues, including rampant government corruption, exacerbated these socio-economic problems. However, senior members of the ruling Movement for Multiparty Democracy (MMD) often placed full blame for the country's problems on the SAP. Government officials also pointed out that the IMF and World Bank harmonised their programmes with Western bilateral donors and used the withdrawal of financial assistance as a tool to ensure compliance with their policy recommendations.[2] Subsequently, the IMF and World Bank's programmes became synonymous with the notions of 'poverty' or 'suffering' in Zambia and expressing hatred for the employees of both institutions became normalised in social discourses.

During the mid-2000s, several politicians capitalised on this history to promote narratives that portrayed Western donors as untrustworthy and encouraged Zambians to fear the conditions underlying their proposal for debt relief under the Highly Indebted Poor Countries (HIPC) Initiative. Patriotic Front (PF) founder, Micheal Sata, employed staged protests, political rallies, radio interviews and coverage in the popular *Post* newspaper to disseminate narratives that suggested the IMF was forcing President Levy Mwanawasa to sell SOEs to foreign investors and that these investors

[1] Peter Henriot, "Retreat of the State: Political Consequences and Social Implications for Zambia," in *Development Review 1997*, ed. Trocaire (Dublin: Trocaire, 1997).

[2] Lise Rakner, *Political and Economic Liberalisation in Zambia 1991–2001* (Uppsala: Nordic Africa Institute, 2003).

would strip the SOEs of their assets and retrench their Zambian workforce. In January 2007, Sata led 4000 protestors to the Ministry of Finance and National Planning, where they presented a petition against the IMF's recommendation for tax increases and the government's sale of 49% of its shares in Zambia National Commercial Bank (ZANACO) to Rabobank of the Netherlands.[3] This protest encouraged University of Zambia (UNZA) students to heckle President Mwanawasa when he visited their institution, while bearing posters that declared the 'IMF takes no interest in Zambia's prosperity' and 'Abash IMF policies for our Zambia'.[4]

Apart from anti-HIPC rhetoric, Sata also promoted narratives that suggested President Mwanawasa and his successor Rupiah Banda were auctioning Zambia's assets to predatory Chinese investors and foreign governments.[5] These narratives enabled the PF to mobilise a large support base and claim victory in the September 2011 general elections. This is in spite of the fact that the debt relief attained from the HIPC Initiative, fiscal discipline, improvements to the investment climate and a rise in global price of copper had facilitated a period of sustained economic growth during the Mwanawasa and Banda eras. Sata's populist election campaign established a model that several political parties have since drawn lessons from or attempted to emulate. However, contemporary politicians tend to use social media to critique the ruling party, share their views about Zambia's economy and engage in debates about its debt burden. News tabloids, radio stations and private television channels often expand their audience by reproducing the statements that are published on social media.

This shift to political campaigning on social media has coincided with the growth in the number of Zambians that use mobile phone internet subscriptions to communicate and share news through platforms such as Facebook, X/Twitter, Tik Tok and WhatsApp.[6] A significant amount of misinformation is being intentionally and unintentionally shared on these

[3] Ng'andu P. Magande, *The Depth of My Footprints* (Atlanta: Maleendo & Company, 2018).

[4] Reuters, "Zambian students jeer president over state bank shares sale to a foreign bank," *Reuters*, 20 January 2007.

[5] Emmanuel Matambo, "A choreographed Sinophobia? An analysis of China's identity from the perspective of Zambia's Patriotic Front," *Africa Review* 12, no. 1 (2020).

[6] Zambia's mobile phone internet penetration rate increased from 49.4 per 100 inhabitants in 2018 to 57.9 per 100 inhabitants in 2023. See Zambia Information and Communications and Technology Authority, *ICT Sector 2024 Mid-Year Market Report* (Lusaka: ZICTA, 2024).

platforms.[7] This misinformation created a number of challenges during the tenure of President Edgar Lungu (2015–2021) and is producing hostility towards the current administration's efforts to restructure Zambia's debt. This chapter will explore social media narratives surrounding the government's attempts to negotiate for an economic bailout package from the IMF and Zambia's emergence as a guinea pig for the Group of Twenty (G20) Common Framework for Debt Treatment.

The Challenge of Securing an Economic Bailout Package

A key priority for the Lungu administration after the August 2016 general elections was securing a US$1.3 billion Extended Credit Facility (ECF) from the IMF to stabilise the economy following a decline in revenues earned from the copper industry. Its negotiations for the ECF contributed to speculation from social media news tabloids that the IMF was going to impose harsh policy conditions and push for the privatisation of SOEs such as Zamtel. These rumours generated public anger and demands that the government looks for an alternative source of financing. This is despite the Minister of Finance, Felix Mutati, clarifying that the IMF's assistance would be based on policy reforms laid out in the government's home-grown economic recovery programme rather than externally generated policies.[8] In June 2017, an IMF spokesperson also refuted what he described as an 'outrageous', 'utterly false' and 'rubbish' report circulating on social media, which alleged that the IMF mission leader, Tsidi Tsikata, had accepted a bribe from Zambian government officials and assured them that he could convince the IMF Executive Board to approve the ECF.[9] National Development Planning Minister, Lucky Mulusa, also criticised social media users for posting negative stories about the government and contended that they were damaging Zambia's ability to attract

[7] Misinformation can be defined as information that is false or misleading because it excludes important contextual details. See Jon Roozenbeek and Sander Van der Linden, *The Psychology of Misinformation* (Cambridge: Cambridge University Press, 2024).

[8] Mwebantu, "Mutati rubbishes rumours of IMF demanding sale of Zamtel," *Facebook*, 1:30 pm, 30 October 2016.

[9] Zambian Watchdog, "Zambia Regime Claims It Bribed IMF Official Tsikata To Secure Loan," Facebook, 08:07 am, 21 June 2017; Gerry Rice, "Transcript of IMF Press Briefing," *IMF Press Centre*, 22 June 2017.

foreign direct investment (FDI) since international media companies such as *Bloomberg* were reproducing their statements.[10]

In August 2018, the Minister of Information and Broadcasting, Dora Siliya, went on X/Twitter to dispute a viral post that had suggested the IMF was withdrawing its Resident Representative, Alfredo Baldini, and that it had no plans to send a replacement.[11] Initially, social media users hypothesised that Baldini's withdrawal was an outcome of the IMF's formal suspension of all negotiations for an ECF or a sign that it had loss of confidence in the Zambian government due to concerns about the widespread embezzlement of public funds. However, news tabloids later revealed that it was the Zambian government that had asked the IMF to recall Baldini because they did not like comments that he had made about their approach to fiscal discipline and the country's debt sustainability.[12] PF party loyalists disputed these claims and used repressive tactics to restrict opposition political parties and private media companies from spreading counternarratives or rumours about the Chinese government's supposed role in Zambia's mounting debt crisis. Nevertheless, debates about the impacts of cheap Chinese infrastructure loans dominated Zambian social media after officials from the USA suggested that China was deliberately seeking to get heavily indebted countries to default and relinquish control of strategic assets they had offered as collateral, such as Zambia Electricity Supply Corporation (ZESCO).[13]

Foreign perceptions about Zambia's economic stability were further damaged by President Lungu's frequent firing and hiring of a new Minister of Finance as well as the dismissal of the respected Bank of Zambia (BoZ) Governor, Denny Kalyalya, in August 2020. These actions led South Africa's then Minister of Finance, Tito Mboweni, to publish a series of X/Twitter posts where he criticised Lungu for firing Kalyalya and vowed to mobilise other people against the decision.[14] The Zambian economy

[10] Mukosha Funga Njenga, "Zambia not desperate for IMF aid- Minister," *News Diggers*, 10 July 2017.

[11] Dora Siliya (@Dora_Siliya), "The IMF is in Zambia for various progs and is not leaving ..." *X/Twitter*, 4:30 pm, 24 August 2018.

[12] The Mast, "IMF Rep's Open Talk on Debt Angered Govt," *Facebook*, 4:39 pm, 28 August 2018.

[13] Africa Confidential, "Bonds, bills and ever bigger debts," *Africa Confidential* 59, no. 18 (2018).

[14] Peter Fabricius, "Mboweni blasts Zambian president for firing the country's central bank governor," *Daily Maverick*, 23 August 2020.

eventually hit a breaking point in November 2020, when the government announced that it was suspending interest payments to its Eurobond holders, making Zambia the first African country to default on its external debt during the COVID-19 pandemic. It is against this backdrop that United Party for National Development (UPND) president, Hakainde Hichilema, began to increasingly use social media to criticise Lungu's management of the economy and argue that his party could quickly secure an ECF from the IMF if it were to win the August 2021 general elections.[15] These social media campaigns and a strong youth turnout are widely credited with helping Hichilema's subsequent victory in these elections.

Shortly after ascending to power, Hichilema reappointed Denny Kalyalya as BoZ Governor and picked the well-regarded Situmbeko Musokotwane to be his Minister of Finance and National Planning. Thereafter, President Hichilema and Musokotwane unveiled their plans for reviving economic growth centred on good governance, debt treatment and financial assistance from the IMF and World Bank.[16] In December 2021, the government attained a staff-level agreement with the IMF for a three-year programme supported by an US$1.3 billion ECF, the IMF Executive Board approved the deal in August 2022 and the World Bank also committed itself to supporting Zambia's homegrown economic programme. These developments were met with positive responses from most Zambian social media users. However, some opposition politicians started to sensitise their social media followers about the SAP and to argue that Zambian voters would cry at the end of the UPND's tenure after feeling the impacts of austerity and the privatisation of SOEs that these multilateral financial institutions would force the government to implement.[17]

[15] Hakainde Hichilema, "We are rescheduling the debt on August 14th after swearing in," *Facebook*, 9:00 am, 16 March 2021; Hakainde Hichilema, "Way Forward on Debt and Default," *Facebook*, 6:24 am, 19 November 2020; Hakainde Hichilema, "Zambia's Request to Suspend Debt Servicing," *Facebook*, 4:46 pm, 22 September 2020.

[16] Hakainde Hichilema, "In our meeting with the International Monetary Fund ...," *Facebook*, 1:54 pm, 24 September 2021.

[17] Saboi Imboela, "HH is a serious capitalist ...," *Facebook*, 7:42 pm, 23 September 2021; Sean E. Tembo, "Does Zambia Really Need an IMF Bailout Loan?," *Facebook*, 5:06 am, 31 August 2021; Azwell Banda, "HH, Musokotwane, UPND and the IMF: propaganda and lies on full display," *Facebook*, 3:35 pm, 29 May 2022; Fred M'membe, "Nipano Tuli: It Will End In Tears," *Facebook*, 4:15 pm, 31 August 2022.

President Hichilema attempted to calm the ensuing public anxiety by emphasising that the IMF and World Bank are interested in supporting Zambia's economy recovery since it is a shareholder in both institutions and their policy recommendations align with domestic development plans.[18] The IMF Managing Director Kristalina Georgieva acknowledged her institution's past mistakes during a town hall meeting with UNZA students and insisted that the IMF had changed its practices through the input of its staff that now come from diverse backgrounds. Georgieva also discussed her lived experiences in Bulgaria to underscore the need for governments to implement tough measures to stabilise an economy.[19] However, these arguments did not quell the growth of anti-IMF rhetoric in social media debates about Zambia's debt crisis.

Zambia Becomes a Guinea Pig

In July 2022, the Zambian government began negotiating for a debt treatment plan with the country's Official Creditor Committee (OCC) that was formed under the G20 Common Framework for Debt Treatment.[20] During this process, President Hichilema often asked representatives from the IMF, World Bank and OCC member countries for their support in ensuring the negotiations are quickly concluded so that Zambia could improve its ability to attract FDI and achieve economic stability. Several Western diplomatic officials and IMF representatives asserted that the negotiations were being drawn out by the Chinese government's lack of institutional capacity to participate in multilateral debt restructuring negotiations and to coordinate its public and private lending institutions.[21] However, the United States Secretary of the Treasury Janet Yellen's remarks elicited the sharpest response from the Chinese

[18] Hakainde Hichilema (@HHichilema), "We own @IFC_org, the government of #Zambia is a shareholder in @WorldBank ..." *X/Twitter*, 4:23 pm, 18 July 2022.

[19] Ministry of Finance & National Planning, "Townhall with Kristalina Georgieva, IMF Managing Director," *Facebook*, 7:58 am, 24 January 2023.

[20] The OCC is comprised of Belgium, China, Denmark, France, India, Israel, Italy, Japan, the Netherlands, Russia, Saudi Arabia, South Africa, Sweden, Switzerland, the United Kingdom and the USA. Representatives from the IMF and World Bank participate as observers.

[21] Judith Malunga, "China slows down Zambia's debt restructuring programme," *News Diggers*, 8 April 2022 2022; Philip Chisalu and Ulande Nkomesha, "It's difficult for China to cut Zambia's debt because it has its own challenges—IMF," *News Diggers*, 25 January 2023.

government, who advised her to focus on the US domestic debt problems and 'to stop sabotaging the efforts that other sovereign countries were making to resolve their debt issues'.[22] The leaders of the PF, Socialist Party (SP) and Patriots for Economic Progress (PeP) responded to this diplomatic storm by demanding that President Hichilema directly petitions the Chinese government for assistance in these negotiations and labelling him a naive puppet of the 'imperialist' West.[23]

Prominent media outlets published these narratives without debunking false statements or pointing out that China is co-chair of the OCC and several press releases from the Ministry of Finance and National Planning and Ministry of Foreign Affairs and International Cooperation had shown Zambian and Chinese officials holding discussions on the restructuring of Zambia's debt. As a result, many Zambians that accessed the narratives pushed by opposition parties believed that the government was firmly pro-West and not engaging in talks with the Chinese government. Although, this did not stop most Zambians and the diplomatic corps from celebrating, with much fanfare, the announcement that the government and OCC had finally agreed on a debt treatment plan in June 2023.[24] Economists and civil society activists provided varied analyses of the opportunities and challenges presented by the agreement on debt treatment. President Hichilema asserted that Zambia's experience with the G20 Common Framework had turned it into a 'guinea pig' on how the debts of other poor countries could be restructured. Hichilema also appealed for diplomatic support to resolve the differences between Zambia's private creditors and the OCC that were delaying the completion of all of its negotiations for debt treatment.

In response, senior members of the PF and SP accused his administration of having engaged in deceptive practices, poor decision-making and

[22] Ulande Nkomesha, "Chinese Embassy Scolds US Envoy: Deal with your own debt, don't sabotage other nations," *News Diggers*, 25 January 2023 2023.

[23] Cynthia M. Kamwengo, "Social Media Debates on Zambia's Evolving Relations with The West and East: Trends and Implications," *Megatrends Policy Brief 21* (2024).

[24] Ministry of Finance & National Planning, "Zambia Reaches Agreement with Official Creditors on Debt Treatment under the G20 Common Framework," 22 June 2023; Nicholas Woolley (@nkwoolley), "Zambia. Ena Wakulekafye..." *X/Twitter*, 23 June 2023; Chinese Embassy in Zambia, "Thanks to the joint efforts of the two heads of state..." *Facebook*, 10:59 am, 23 June 2023.

deliberately sabotaging the restructuring of Zambia's debt.[25] These political parties also accused the government of financial misconduct and of lacking a clear development vision on every occasion that it announced the contraction of new loans from bilateral or multilateral partners to support the implementation of its homegrown economic programme. The notion that the IMF is dictating government policy and forcing it to sale SOEs has also remained a reoccurring theme in these debates. This includes a statement PF president, Miles Sampa, posted on Facebook in August 2024, which alleged that the IMF was pressuring the government to remove the Republican President from the Industrial Development Corporation (IDC) board of directors and to sell its assets such as the Mulungushi International Conference Centre.[26] The IMF Resident Representative, Eric Lautier, refuted Sampa's claims and expressed frustration at the fact that Zambian politicians tend to promote economic arguments that cannot be backed by factual evidence. However, Sampa countered that Lautier was a clueless economic elite who did not understand the needs of poor Zambians.[27]

Opposition political parties have also constructed themselves as true patriots and made repeated calls to action for their social media followers to save Zambia by voting for them instead of Hichilema's UPND in the 2026 general elections.[28] These populist social media campaigns tend to offer simplistic solutions to Zambia's complex economic problems, such as the need to employ local human resources instead of foreign technical assistance. It is not clear to what extent these narratives will impact voting behaviour in the 2026 general elections. However, opposition political parties will continue to use them to successfully mobilise a support base as long as media outlets and academics do not make a sufficient effort to debunk false narratives.

[25] Fred M'membe, "Zambia A Guinea Pig?," *Facebook*, 7:14 am, 23 March 2024; Emmanuel Mwamba, "Earlier Debt Restructuring success was Sabotaged by President Hichilema and his officials," *Facebook*, 2:20 pm, 27 January 2024.

[26] Miles Sampa, "Government through IDC want to sell...," *Facebook*, 2:09 pm, 13 August 2024.

[27] Philip Chisalu, "IMF denies pressuring govt, IDC to sell assets," *News Diggers*, 16 August 2024 2024; Miles Sampa, "About The IMF Representative in Zambia Eric Lautier & The Cake Syndrome." *Facebook*, 11:57 am, 16 August 2024.

[28] Kamwengo, "Social Media Debates on Zambia's Evolving Relations with The West and East: Trends and Implications."

Conclusion

The Zambian government's recent efforts to restructure the country's foreign debt has encountered domestic resistance due to political campaigns by opposition parties that have resurrected public memory of the SAP and distrust of bilateral and multilateral partners. President Hichilema has stated on several occasions that he intends to modify local perspectives so that Zambians become accountable for their role in accruing debt and making the economy resilient to external shocks.[29] Official government communications teams have also used press conferences live streamed on local television stations, radio programmes and social media platforms to clarify misinformation about Zambia's path to debt treatment. These perspectives are not always accessible to international audiences, which has made some observers susceptible to publishing misinformation.[30] These challenges underscore the need for all stakeholders to engage in fact checking and an examination of the historical context of debates about Zambia's political economy.

References

Africa Confidential. "Bonds, Bills and Ever Bigger Debts." *Africa Confidential* 59, no. 18. (2018). https://www.africa-confidential.com/article-preview/id/12424/Bonds%2c_bills_and_ever_bigger_debts.

Banda, Azwell. "HH, Musokotwane, UPND and the IMF: Propaganda and Lies on Full Display." *Facebook*, 3:35pm, 29 May 2022. https://www.facebook.com/themastzambia/posts/pfbid024uaycRaxHw1pcoAHmDuXaFQnfoBzuwmZCH6V7fmpohtTyimiT1TVqwEJyM2PDjrFl.

Chinese Embassy in Zambia. "Thanks to the Joint Efforts of the Two Heads of State..." *Facebook*, 10:59am, 23 June 2023. https://www.facebook.com/permalink.php?story_fbid=pfbid02PNNQpb938ykYcHYGEjp5ZvbbnoYHBb2WEBjzEFuKL4svQ8USB5gAv3mjFfsVWKcel&id=100069399120744.

Chisalu, Philip. "IMF Denies Pressuring Govt, IDC to Sell Assets." *News Diggers*, 16 August 2024.

[29] Hakainde Hichilema, "Meeting with the British High Commissioner" (Lusaka, State House, 11 June 2024); Hakainde Hichilema, "Remarks made during courtesy call by World Bank Country Director Nathan Belete" (Lusaka, State House, 27 June 2023).

[30] For example, opposition political parties used a viral Bloomberg story that indicated that Zambia had 'erroneously' made a US$80 million debt payment to China to fuel anti-government sentiment. See Taonga Mitimingi and Matthew Hill, "Zambia remedying $80 million erroneous debt payment to China," *Bloomberg*, 9 December 2024.

Chisalu, Philip, and Ulande Nkomesha. "It's Difficult for China to Cut Zambia's Debt Because It Has Its Own Challenges – IMF." *News Diggers*, 25 January 2023.

Zambia Information Communications and Technology Authority. *ICT Sector 2024 Mid-Year Market Report*. Lusaka: ZICTA, 2024.

Fabricius, Peter "Mboweni Blasts Zambian President for Firing the Country's Central Bank Governor." *Daily Maverick*, 23 August 2020. https://www.dailymaverick.co.za/article/2020-08-23-mboweni-blasts-zambian-president-for-firing-the-countrys-central-bank-governor/.

Henriot, Peter. "Retreat of the State: Political Consequences and Social Implications for Zambia." In *Development Review 1997*, edited by Trocaire, 39-60. Dublin: Trocaire, 1997.

Hichilema, Hakainde. "In Our Meeting with the International Monetary Fund...," *Facebook*, 1:54pm, 24 September 2021a. https://www.facebook.com/hakainde.hichilema/posts/pfbid0k7iv4QW9ZFr2gyDUfdMqPN3HZo9j497veAUgeuAnEAFSMak3qHFnYiCnq5pAJAt3l.

———. "Meeting with the British High Commissioner." Lusaka: State House, 11 June 2024.

———. "Remarks made during courtesy call by World Bank Country Director Nathan Belete." Lusaka: State House, 27 June 2023.

———. "Way Forward on Debt and Default." *Facebook*, 6:24am, 19 November 2020a, 2020. https://www.facebook.com/hakainde.hichilema/posts/pfbid0R5WBSM8oNBFFaZpsu2wEeACJPVEjEdW69ec4mvmqQBEKyBEUJAVEdmrdbUYRmgFMl.

———. "We Are Rescheduling the Debt on August 14th after Swearing In." *Facebook*, 9:00am, 16 March 2021b, 2021. https://www.facebook.com/hakainde.hichilema/posts/we-are-rescheduling-the-debt-on-august-14th-after-swearing-in-this-measure-will-/296586065157461/.

———. "We Own @Ifc_Org, the Government of #Zambia Is a Shareholder in @ Worldbank..." *X/Twitter*, 4:23pm, 18 July 2022. https://twitter.com/HHichilema/status/1549052268208459776.

———. "Zambia's Request to Suspend Debt Servicing." *Facebook*, 4:46pm, 22 September 2020b, 2020. https://www.facebook.com/hakainde.hichilema/posts/pfbid034bjT7gqdZ7MHhaND8ND6sNBrEJCaLSdb93as7wED2h9QVaQwR4EPNq4XnLJdbMcxl.

Imboela, Saboi. "HH Is a Serious Capitalist...," *Facebook*, 7:42pm, 23 September 2021, https://www.facebook.com/saboi.imboela.9/posts/pfbid05i79odc6p12ujg9CAGLjo8AY5d4RFFg8CpigCkext1PhfJt63pvNx3WUYmxXPjCxl.

Kamwengo, Cynthia M. "Social Media Debates on Zambia's Evolving Relations with the West and East: Trends and Implications." *Megatrends Policy Brief 21* (2024). https://doi.org/10.18449/2024MTA-PB21.

M'membe, Fred. "Nipano Tuli: It Will End in Tears." *Facebook*, 4:15pm, 31 August 2022. https://www.facebook.com/DrFredMmembe/posts/pfbid02rsVjZcVLEEFwy1W3zHp3vPqzgatiWKnYUoqBuRfgcYHAbtrEte-VHGGNXUcNuYrhLl.

———. "Zambia a Guinea Pig?" *Facebook*, 7:14am, 23 March 2024. https://www.facebook.com/DrFredMmembe/videos/937415661013137.

Magande, Ng'andu P. *The Depth of My Footprints*. Atlanta: Maleendo & Company, 2018.

Malunga, Judith. "China Slows Down Zambia's Debt Restructuring Programme." *News Diggers*, 8 April 2022 2022.

Matambo, Emmanuel. "A Choreographed Sinophobia? An Analysis of China's Identity from the Perspective of Zambia's Patriotic Front." *Africa Review* 12, no. 1 (2020): 92-112.

Ministry of Finance & National Planning. "Townhall with Kristalina Georgieva, IMF Managing Director." *Facebook*, 7:58am, 24 January 2023. https://www.facebook.com/zambiafinanceministry/videos/1823669404662338/.

"Zambia Reaches Agreement with Official Creditors on Debt Treatment under the G20 Common Framework." 22 June 2023, https://www.mofnp.gov.zm/?p=7444.

Mitimingi, Taonga, and Matthew Hill. "Zambia Remedying $80 Million Erroneous Debt Payment to China." *Bloomberg*, 9 December 2024. https://www.bloomberg.com/news/articles/2024-12-09/zambia-remedying-80-million-erroneous-debt-payment-to-china.

Mwamba, Emmanuel. "Earlier Debt Restructuring Success Was Sabotaged by President Hichilema and His Officials." *Facebook*, 2:20pm, 27 January 2024. https://www.facebook.com/emmanuel.mwamba.35/posts/pfbid0bp9Jk6moVFJB1dHEd1ducuPPNgZE6JajPRFAL9eJFDFe52DGGP-sZ4CtqYGqp4kC1l.

Mwebantu. "Mutati Rubbishes Rumours of IMF Demanding Sale of Zamtel." *Facebook*, 1:30pm, 30 October 2016. https://www.facebook.com/photo/?fbid=1104245766362184&set=a.247946581992111.

Njenga, Mukosha Funga. "Zambia Not Desperate for IMF Aid- Minister." *News Diggers*, 10 July 2017.

Nkomesha, Ulande. "Chinese Embassy Scolds Us Envoy: Deal with Your Own Debt, Don't Sabotage Other Nations." *News Diggers*, 25 January 2023.

Rakner, Lise. *Political and Economic Liberalisation in Zambia 1991-2001*. Uppsala: Nordic Africa Institute, 2003.

Reuters. "Zambian Students Jeer President over State Bank Shares Sale to a Foreign Bank." *Reuters*, 20 January 2007. https://reuters.screenocean.com/record/439089.

Rice, Gerry. "Transcript of IMF Press Briefing." *IMF Press Centre*, 22 June 2017, https://www.imf.org/en/News/Articles/2017/06/22/tr062217-transcript-of-imf-press-briefing.

Roozenbeek, Jon, and Sander Van der Linden. *The Psychology of Misinformation*. Cambridge: Cambridge University Press, 2024.

Sampa, Miles. "Government through IDC Want to Sell...," *Facebook*, 2:09pm, 13 August 2024a, 2024. https://www.facebook.com/msampa1/posts/pfbid0796Hxe2gSLcNio97HkySRdsXpQk2ZBD6zQGBBWu3jmc5v-vW8y8DWk8MxH7tJJboRl.

——— " About The IMF Representative in Zambia Eric Lautier & The Cake Syndrome." *Facebook*, 11:57am, 16 August 2024b. https://www.facebook.com/msampa1/posts/pfbid02zzY3ZZkTptqAwzH1wp3uH1AyJxH7Tf5K-NUTmyW3rwV81WCeDHPZPA9AY8Kwjvujdl.

Siliya, Dora. "The IMF is in Zambia for various progs and is not leaving...," *X/Twitter*, 4:30pm, 24 August 2018. https://x.com/Dora_Siliya/status/1033013805670912000.

Tembo, Sean E. "Does Zambia Really Need an IMF Bailout Loan?" Facebook, 5:06am, 31 August 2021. https://www.facebook.com/PePpresidentSET/posts/pfbid034LNG5TKG9BkLoHeYtqhoRdNNzsV95doiYf1mo19R-A3GHFa33p1Fj9p6LYfddnznpl.

The Mast. "IMF Rep's Open Talk on Debt Angered Govt." *Facebook*, 4:39pm, 28 August 2018. https://www.facebook.com/themastzambia/posts/pfbid027zdsjg3jxgWFWgA5EAE5JYToieM5vrimEqyBERcyU-zuk8553roBzyJ6qkb1V7Ljol.

Woolley, Nicholas. "Zambia. Ena Wakulekafye...," *X/Twitter*, 11:07am, 23 June 2023. https://x.com/nkwoolley/status/1672184670396579843.

Zambian Watchdog. Zambia Regime Claims It Bribed IMF Official Tsikata to Secure Loan. *Facebook*, 08:07am, 21 June 2017. https://www.facebook.com/photo/?fbid=1553578861359525&set=a.574571859260235.

CHAPTER 10

The Development of Zambian Civil Society Over the Last 20 Years with Special Reference to the Patriotic Front (PF) Years

McDonald Chipenzi

Abstract Debt was incurred as a feature of the years of the Lungu Presidency. But the presidency had also to deal with a growing non-governmental sector. Civil society was monitored and efforts were made to constrain its free comments on a range of issues, including what was happening in the economy.

Keywords Civil society • Organisational difficulties • Threats of arrest

> If you don't like something, change it. If you can't change it, change your attitude.

Catch words:

'Civil Society' is defined by the Constitution of Zambia in Article 266, to mean 'a group of persons, who are not part of the Government, who associate for the purpose of advancing or protecting particular interests' while the National Policy on Non-Governmental Organisations (NGOs) (2018) by the Ministry of Community Development and Social Services for Zambia,

---

The original version of the chapter has been revised. A correction to this chapter can be found at https://doi.org/10.1007/978-3-031-93030-0_11

S. Chan, *The Economic Transformation and Political Economy of Zambia*, Palgrave Studies in African and Development Economics,
https://doi.org/10.1007/978-3-031-93030-0_10

defines 'civil Society' (CS) to mean to 'the arena outside of the family, the state and the market which is created by individuals and collective actions, organisations and institutions to advance shared interests'.

'Non-Governmental Organisation' (NGO) is defined as 'Private voluntary grouping of individuals or associations, whether corporate or unincorporated, not established or operated for profit, partisan politics or any commercial purposes and whom or which have organised themselves for the promotion of civic education, advocacy, human rights, social welfare, development, charity, research or other activity or programme for the benefit or interest of the public through resources mobilised from sources within or outside Zambia' (NGO Act No. 16 of 2009).

***Political Party: the Constitution defines a** 'political party' means 'an association whose objectives include the contesting of elections in order to form government or influence the policy of the national or local government'.*

Introduction

Zambia earned an undisputed reputation in the Southern African Development Council (SADC) region as one of the continent's most stable democracies ever since its transition to multiparty rule over a generation of years ago. During the period, Zambia saw a sprawling civil society movement emerging in all sectors, albeit environmental, socio-economic, cultural, governance, education, gender and political. Many of the civil society organisations that emerged around the 1980s and 1990s were in philanthropic service delivery sector with a few in governance and human rights. In human rights, democracy and governance, prominent one were Zambia National Women's Lobby Group (ZNWLG) then, Foundation For Democratic Process (FODEP), Zambia Monitoring Team (ZIMT), among others.

Around 2000s, there was an emergency, existence and growth of an organised and effective civil society/non-governmental organisation (NGO) movement in the country post the One Party Participatory Democratic Political System under the founding President Kenneth Kaunda's regime. This was one of the greatest social phenomena to have had happened in the country in the latter part of the twentieth century and, certainly, in the first and second millennia.

Historic Background

With the dawn of multiparty democracy in many other countries including Zambia in the 1990s and part of the 2000s, and as observed by Sfeir-Younis, civil society organisations (CSOs) grew in size and numbers becoming 'instrumental in granting power and voice to many people who are poor, voiceless and powerless and a medium through which these sections of society can express their opinions, views, and possible strategic concerns' on any public affair and/or policies.[1] However, in many instances, civil society/NGO sector determines, shapes, sets and develops national agenda and puts the ruling political parties and governments on their toes during their reign. For governments and civil society/NGOs to act and engage effectively in addressing challenges facing humanity and reshape today and the future, inclusivity, collaborative, consultative and involvement strategies must be devised for broad-based agreed policy making/formulation and implementation. Some scholars have argued strongly that to propose a paradigm shift in a world that moves rapidly in favour of all forms of fundamentalisms may be seen as an oxymoronic proposition. Nonetheless, Sfeir-Younis concludes that 'as we shift towards a new paradigm, policy will have to change accordingly. This change demands significant shifts in the role of civil society.' Arguably, the measure of democratic tolerance in any country is observable through how its leaders treat and perceive the role of governance and human rights-oriented civil society/NGOs and its leaders.

In the period under review to which this chapter is dedicated to speak, the PF regime determinedly engaged with its might and efforts to shrink the democratic space (SDS) of civil society by restricting their freedom of speech, association, movement and assembly.[2]

The year was 2011 when the pioneer political party in the re-introduction of multiparty democracy—the Movement for Multiparty Democracy (MMD)—was dislodged from political and state power after being on the political saddle for two decades (20 years). The decade long opposition party rival—Patriotic Front (PF)—under stewardship of a populist leader—late Michael Sata—democratically usurped the political and state power from MMD and Rupiah Banda, respectively, with a 43% vote win against the incumbent then, Rupiah Bwezani Banda popularly known as RB who got 36%. Immediately President Sata assumed power; the outside observers and local activists converged in opinion and conclusion that the country's tradition of being a glowing democracy was under serious threat. In addition, the PF party constitution envisaged a government including mass movements that would be run by 'faithful members of the

[1] Sfeir-Younis, 2004: 29.
[2] Action Aid Zambia, 2019.

party'.[3] This resulted into the politicisation of the government and mass movements. As a result those who did not agree or seen to be 'faithful members' of the party suffered discrimination, marginalisation and labelling. This contributed to the restrictive civic, media and political environment and constant attacks on freedom of expression and association on such individuals and their institutions. Consequently, there was rapid assault, with impunity, on civil society and political opponents. Political and civil society rallies/assemblies were a nightmare during the 10-year reign of the PF.

To demonstrate this, in April 2012, the entire opposition leadership in the country had to fly to and held a media conference in South Africa just because it was not attainable in Zambia at the time. Common Wealth Secretary-General Patricia Scotland had to fly in the country to appreciate the happenings of the time. Worse still, after the demise of President Sata in 2014, which was followed by the assumption of state power by his successor from the same political party—President Edgar Chagwa Lungu—after a disputed presidential election held in 2015, the country saw an upsurge in tyrannical tendencies resulting into him (President Lungu) declaring a State of Threatened Emergency in 2017. This declaration meant restricted civil liberties and rights of most Zambians, especially the perceived political and civic opponents. The Zambian church, then, warned that the country was 'not far from being a dictatorship, if not already a dictator', while the following year, 2018, political scientists Bratton, Dulani and Nkomo concluded that 'the country faces a choice of the future between democratic deepening and authoritarian backsliding'.[4]

Clearly, the unfolding political events at the time were oblivious of the fact that the civic and political spaces civil society and citizens supposed to enjoy were enshrined in the republican Constitution despite the craw-back clauses. These freedoms were hard-won product by the country's ancestors involved in anti-colonial struggles then and had been key to the progress made since then towards overcoming poverty, social justice and exclusion in the country. Convergingly, Amnesty International (AI) observed two years later in 2021, the 'conspicuously shrinking civic and political spaces'.[5] In its report titled '*Zambia: Ruling by fear and repression*' that in the past few years (2011–2021), AI observed that Zambia's

[3] PF Constitution, Art 3, 2001.
[4] Action Aid-Zambia (AAZ), 2019.
[5] Amnesty International (AI), 2021.

human rights situation had deteriorated remarkably. Ordinary people, civil society and opposition political party supporters and leaders increasingly were subjected to a restrictive environment where they were unable to freely assemble publicly, protest, demonstrate or engage in public demonstrations or protest against government actions without being subjected to intimidation, harassment and violence by ruling party supporters popularly called cadres and the police. Self-censorship on what one does or says during this period was a common adopted strategy by everyone. By-elections were bloody and CSOs participating in these by-elections as observers and monitors suffered similar attacks. Fearing against reprisals, many people, civil society, church, ordinary people and the media resorted to silent protests waiting for the day of the general election to vent their anger, which they demonstrated on 12 August 2021 by voting out the regime.

In addition, instead of repealing archaic laws that endangered existence of civil society, the laws were even tightened and new ones such as the cyber Security and Cyber Crimes Act were hastily enacted, within 10 days, to further suppress citizens' rights to assemblies on social media platforms such as WhatsApp, Facebook now X, among others, through state monitoring, surveillance and interception of citizens' conversations and communication. The levels and incidences of civil society oppression and suppression during the period under review were unprecedented since the re-introduction of plural politics in Zambia in 1991. It was the first time, after a generation into plural politics, that the country degenerated and witnessed such kind of political intolerance, violence, ethnic marginalisation and discrimination. In this regard, many civil society leaders and activists were threatened with deregistration, intimidated, harassed, politically tagged/labelled and excluded, marginalised, discriminated and arrested. All those who tried to champion human rights and good governance during the period were labelled as agents of imperialists—Western governments—and allies of the main opposition political party—the United Party for National Development (UPND)—now the current ruling party.

Therefore, as aptly summarised by the United Nations Special Rapporteur on Freedom of Expression and Opinion, Irene Khan,[6] in her preliminary observation in the 2025 assessment of the country's human rights situation focused on Freedom of Expression and Opinion, opined:

[6] Irene Khan, 2025.

> The 2021 Presidential elections in Zambia marked a significant political transition with the victory of the United Party for National Development (UPND), and an end to the decade long rule of the Patriotic Front (PF) during which grave human rights violations and high levels of political violence prevailed with impunity. Freedom of expression was a major casualty during those years. Opposition leaders, activists, human rights defenders and journalists were attacked, jailed or killed, at least two prominent independent media outlets shut down, and civic space severely restricted.

The current President, himself (Hakainde Hichilema) and many senior members of his government were targets of human rights violations. This chapter discusses the Development of Zambian Civil Society over the last 10 years of the Patriotic Front (PF) reign under the stewardship of Late President Michael Chilufya Sata and later under President Edgar Chagwa Lungu. The reign started in 2011 when the PF swept to power after being in opposition for 10 years (2001–2011). However, in 2014, the PF founding and republican President then, Michael Chilufya Sata, passed on triggering a presidential election which was held in 2015. PF candidate Edgar Chagwa Lungu was declared winner of the 2015 Presidential Election with a narrow margin against his rival Hakainde Hichilema of the United Party for National Development (UPND). This disputed presidential opened a new political chapter in the country that affected the operations of civil society organisations in the country.

Identified Operational Challenges for Civil Society During the PF Reign

The main challenges in the operations of the civil society identified during the PF government era towards the growth of the civil Society were intolerance levels exhibited by the ruling party and the government to divergent views offered by the civil society. This led to heightened restrictions in the enjoyment of the fundamental freedom of assembly, expression and opinion, speech, association and movement and protests and demonstrations by the civil society organisations perceived to be aligned to the opposition UPND. Other challenges included threats of deregistration and cancellation of certificates of Registration, donor withdrawal of funding to NGOs that were not allegedly compliant to the registration demands of the government and also intimidation, marginalisation and discrimination based on alleged partisan alignment of certain civil society organisations and the leadership. A number of civil society leaders were arrested, went into self-exile and resigned to fate for trying to enjoy the fundamental rights provided for in the Constitution of the Republic of Zambia.

The new government in 2011 came to power under the pretext of fulfilling its campaign promises such as delivering a new Constitution, review of the NGO Act, lower taxes and more money in people's pockets within 90 days. This caused pressure on the new government as the 90 days approached and passed without any delivery on the campaigns promise. As more citizens and institutions demanded and held the new government accountable on its promises, the more it became intolerant and restrictive.

Illustratively, *on 12 December 2012, Minister for Justice Wynter Kabimba, who also doubled as the ruling party Secretary-General and in charge of the newly launched Technical Committee on Drafting the New Zambian Constitution, wrote a letter warning those who sensitised citizens to demand the delivery of the new constitution in 90 days as per campaign promise to stop any form of public dialogue meetings/forums or face the wrath of the police. The ministerial letter to the Young African Leaders' Initiative (YALI) read thus:*

> *I refer to the above matter and in particular my letter to your office dated 3rd October 2012, a copy of which is enclosed herewith for your easy reference. In the post newspaper edition dated Monday, 10th December 2012, I read an article attributed to your organisation entitled "YALI urges a constitution Zambians will be proud of". The said article was referring to a provincial dialogue forum which YALI held in Kasama over the Constitutional Making Process. I have made inquiries with the Technical Committee on the Drafting Constitution about your forum and my findings are that the same was not held and/or connected under the auspice of the Committee. Your action was, therefore, in complete defiance of the government decision as contained in my letter referred to above. In view of the above, and by copy of this letter,* ***am informing the Inspector General of Police to take stern action, in future, against anybody from your organisation who shall organise or conduct such a forum outside the supervision of the Technical Committee … I hope you shall heed this timely piece of advice*** *… Wynter Kabimba, Minister of Justice.*

The YALI leadership responded to the Minister Kabimba thus:

Dear Hon. Minister,

RE: THREAT OF ARRESTS EMANATING FROM THE CONDUCT OF PROVINCIAL YOUTH DIALOGUE ON THE CONSTITUTION

We are in receipt of your letter dated 12th December 2012 addressed to our Governance Advisor regarding your misgivings on YALI's position to conduct dialogues on Zambia's Constitution Reform process and your instructions to the Zambia Police Force Inspector General to potentially arrest anybody from our organization who shall organize or conduct such forum outside the supervision of the Technical Committee.

Our Board has reviewed your correspondence and notes with sadness that you, as learned counsel, are failing to appreciate provisions of the Constitution of Zambia which guarantees fundamental freedoms and rights of citizens to freely assemble, participate in public activities and determine laws that govern their lives without government coercion. You will note that the Provincial Dialogue you referred to is not a parallel workshop on the constitutional making process but one of the many interventions by citizens of this Republic who wish to engage in our country's Constitutional reform process.

The Technical Committee, which is now working under intense pressure from your office, was informed of the same dialogue and they sent apologies for their inability to attend our dialogue. An invitation was later extended to the Town Clerk in Kasama, the Committee's District Facilitator who delegated his deputy also mentioned in the Post story.

At this point, we would like to state as follows:

1. *Your threat of "stern action"—be it arrests by the Inspector General of Police who, no doubt, has no autonomy and works at the mercy and convenience of the appointing authority and politicians like you—is unfounded and has no basis in law as YALI is not committing any offense when it decides to hold forums with young leaders on the constitution. We stand ready to defend the rights of fellow citizens and our own rights to engage in the process without any interference from politicians.*
2. *The Technical Committee and the Constitution-making process, which will gobble over K110billion, is funded by taxpayers money and resources gifted by the international community. It goes, therefore, that taxpayers have a constitutional right to engage in this process. There would be no reason at all for this process to continue receiving any support if Government has positioned itself to control how people engage in this process by use of the Technical Committee. YALI will therefore be left without any option but lobby Members of Parliament and the*

International Community to rethink funding to this fraudulent process whose outcome seems to be already predetermined. Your appointment to that office, we now believe is serving to frustrate the constitutional reform process as your immediate predecessor exhibited political willingness for this process to be people-driven.

3. *Undeterred by your threats, YALI will continue to hold its activities which are legal and we are prepared to use all available legal means to defend the right of our young citizens to participate in this process. Should your directive pose any further threat for young citizens to have a say in the process, we are ready to seek an injunction to restrain the Technical Committee from holding its activities in exclusion of our voices as citizens to contribute towards a people-driven constitution. We may further seek a review of your decision in our courts of law which we feel is arbitrary and made without consultations with stakeholders.*

Finally, Hon. Minister, there is need for you to make a clear distinction in the manner in which you want to run Party affairs from your public responsibilities in that honorable office of Minister of Justice. It is, however, in our country's best interest that you restrain yourself, put Zambia first and be impartial in discharging your duties and serve all our peoples. It will not help any Zambian to have a popularly, legitimately and democratically elected Government practice dictatorial tendencies and unleash our men and women in uniform on citizens who exercise their democratic right.

We hope you are satisfied with our response.

Yours faithfully

YOUNG AFRICAN LEADERS INITIATIVE

Andrew Ntewewe

President

Using the Public Order Act that regulated public assemblies and procession, the PF regime exploited its provisions and restricted assemblies and protests during its time in power. During this period, all seminars and gatherings held in hotels and churches were considered illegal and unlawful assemblies. If so how and where? If it is at some strategic installations a charge of attempting to commit a felony is appropriate. For instance, on 29 December, 2019, police arrested Chama Fumba a.k.a. Pilato from a church building in the tourist town of Livingstone's Libuyu area and quickly moved to Livingstone Central Police Station, where he was charged with unlawful assembly before being detained. However, Pilato's docket could not be handed over to the NPA (National Prosecutions

Authority) because the charge of 'unlawful assembly' did not make sense since he was arrested alone, leaving the youths he was addressing at the Catholic Church's Youth Training Centre. Can one person unlawfully assemble? 'Unlawful assembly' means 'a gathering of persons' and not a person in this case one Pilato, without police permit. The arresting officers should have picked all or at least more than ten people that attended his meeting. The PF faithfuls blew the whistle of his (Pilato's) meeting. Those who went to visit Pilato, namely Bonwell Mwewa and Laura Miti, from a civil society organisation Alliance for Community Action (ACA) were arrested also on alleged charge of assaulting the police officer. Magistrate Michael Mulalelo gave duo bail of K2000, each on condition that they presented two sureties each. Miiti and Mwewa allegedly assaulted Woman Constable Fredah Simasho and Directive Inspector Ephraim Silwamba, respectively, on 22 December when they went to visit Pilato at the Livingstone Central Police Station at night, contrary to Section 250 (b) of the Penal Code Chapter 8 of the Laws of Zambia.

Protests were also restricted as demonstrated on June 2020 when Zambian riot police were deployed all over Lusaka, armed and wore full body armour to disperse a youth protest planned and organised in response to several government corruption scandals, but the protesters never arrived at the planned venue but the protest went ahead. In response to Police hunt for the youths, Chama Fumba retorted 'we had this idea. Let's announce that the protest was on. But then let's do it from the bush.' This was done at the last minute. The organisers had told their supporters to stay at home. From an undisclosed location just outside of Lusaka, 13 youth activists live-streamed themselves, making fiery speeches that railed against corruption and poor governance. And, while the police searched fruitlessly for a demonstration that was not happening, more than half a million people tuned in online. 'It has the potential to change how protest will be conducted. There are two streets. There are these physical streets and social media streets. I think this had more influence than if we'd gone to the physical streets.'

There was another upside: no one was shot, beaten or arrested, Fumba a.k.a. Pilato noted. However, a furious police spokesperson announced and assured the public that arrests would be made against the protesters since they protested without police permit—although it's unclear what anyone could be charged with. As one joker noted on social media, 'not entirely accurately, only the Zambia Wildlife Authority has jurisdiction in the bush'. Information Minister and government spokesperson Dora

Siliya confirmed that the police presence in Lusaka on 26 June 2020 was designed to deter an illegal protest. 'The youth have nothing to fear from government. But when they want to gather, in the middle of a pandemic (COVID-19) ... if it was not in a pandemic, I promise you it would be a different story,' she said. 'Even Parliament is not allowed to gather.' Commenting on the same protest, Laura Miti, a veteran activist and head of the Alliance for Community Action, hailed the activists' strategic acumen. 'It was a wonderful ruse,' she said. 'It was two wins — they were heard widely, and they left power with egg all over their faces. Young people feel very invigorated.' The government, on the other hand, must be rattled, said Miti. 'These protests and Malawi together cannot make for a very comfortable situation for the government.' This bush protest was used by the protesters to present a youth charter for the advancement of 'a free society in which every Zambian can aspire for and attain a decent living for themselves'. Its nine central demands include better and more employment; action against corruption; respect for basic freedoms and human rights; accountable leadership; respect for the Constitution; improved education standards; access to health, good housing and sanitation for all; the promotion of women's rights; and a fairer tax system where the rich pay their fair share.

The legal regime was not spared in being used as a tool to restrict the operations of the NGOs in the country. The main ones were the Public Order Act (1955) and the NGO Act No. 16 of 2009 was the most used and controversial piece of legislation or law ever regarding the civic space restriction against the NGOs/CSOs. The non-governmental organisations' (NGO) Act No. 16 of 2009 was enacted by the Zambia Parliament on the 26th of August 2009 (PRMC, 2017). The major objectives of this Act are to:

(i) Provide for the coordination and regulation of NGOs.
(ii) Establish the Non-Governmental Organisations' Registration Board (the NGO Board) and the Zambia Congress of Non-Governmental Organisations (the Congress) and
(iii) Enhance transparency, accountability and performance of non-governmental organisations;
(iv) Align the work of the NGOs to the government's National Development Plans and provide sanctions against erring NGOs.

On 13 September 2013, in its continued threats on CSOs, the PF government, through the then Minister of Community Development Mother and Child Health, Joseph Katema, warned and wrote warning letters[7] to several non-governmental organisations (NGOs), directing them to re-register with the NGO Act No. 16 of 2009 or risked deregistration and be rendered non-operational, adding that all NGOs should register under the 2009 Act of Parliament even if they had other licences or registration certificates from other registration and regulatory authorities for them to be allowed to continue operating.

In May 2014, another letter[8] was written by the Registrar for NGOs under the Ministry of Community Development, Mother and Child Health and reads in part as follows:

> *As you may be aware, the extended period of registration announced by the Minister for Community Development, Mother and Child Health expired on 5th May, 2014. Under this period all existing NGOs were expected to register under the provisions of the NGO Act No. 16 of 2009, section 35(1, 2). We note that despite this extension being made available, your organisation has knowingly failed or neglected to register or commence the registration process with the department of registrar for NGOs. The NGO Act further prohibits persons from operating organisations that are not registered in accordance with the Act (section 19). You are, therefore given thirty days (with effective from receipt of this letter) to show cause why your organisation should not be de-registered for non-compliance with the Act. Awaiting to hear from you. Registrar S, Phiri.*

Take-away from the Registrar's letter were that the NGOs were given a 30-day ultimatum to re-register or be deregistered. In reaction, Foundation for Democratic Process (FODEP) through its Executive Director, then, McDonald Chipenzi, argued his organisation's disinterest to re-register itself under the NGO Act; it deemed the said draconian law and assured government of its readiness to face the consequences in its defence for civil and political rights.[9] 'We are for and equal to the challenge,' Chipenzi assured government. The organisation's argument anchored on the premise that it was legally registered under the Societies Act (1968) and the NGO Act was not superior to the Societies Act under which the organisation was registered. This triggered a court process commenced by seven

[7] Government letter to NGOs dated 13 September 2013.

[8] Registrar for NGOs' letter to NGOs date 12 May 2014.

[9] Zambia Eye, June 2014.

NGOs led by FODEP under the leadership of Mr. Chipenzi. This prompted the government to reverse its hard stance not to review the controversial NGO Act and allowed the NGOs to remain registered under the laws they were registered and continue to operate as usual.

The PF government through its spokesperson, late Mwansa Kapeya assured the NGOs of the government's desire and willingness to undertake a review process on the Non-Governmental Organisation (NGO) Act of 2009 while it was being implemented but recognised the concerns raised by some NGOs regarding some legal impediments within the new NGO Act that needed to be addressed. He said since the NGO Act was already an enacted law which needed to be implemented and adhered to in its current form, government had commenced the registration process of the NGOs on the basis of those willing to register under the new law as a way of operationalising the Act while the review process followed. 'Government wishes to make its position clear on the registration of NGOs under the NGO Act No 16 of 2009. This is in the wake of concerns raised by some NGOs over the operationalisation of the Act. First and foremost, Government wishes to amplify the commitment it attaches to NGOs as partners in supplementing its efforts in development,' Mr. Kapeya said. On the decision by the NGOs to approach the courts over the decision by the government to force NGOs to re-register under the NGO Act and migrate to the NGO Registration Board, late Kapeya argued that it was the duty of the Courts to interpret whether the law in question was bad and that, at the moment, government was of the view that the sentiments being made on the NGO Act by some stakeholders were 'mere speculation' as no one had been injured by the said law so far despite donors threatening to suspend funding to NGOs that were not registered under the Act.

The, then, Vice-Chairperson-Council of NGOs—a statutory body to coordinate the work and operation of the NGOs in Zambia—McDonald Chipenzi, who was also FODEP Executive Director, assured the NGO fraternity that government and the non-governmental organisations (NGOs) agreed to review the NGO Act No. 26 of 2009 to bring to rest the contentious issues observed by the stakeholders. The decision was arrived at following the fruitful discussion held with the NGOs, the then Justice Minister and Attorney General. Mr. Chipenzi said the parties also agreed to suspend the punitive measures that government had put in place to compel NGOs to migrate from the Societies Act or any other registration office to the NGO Department under the NGO Registration Board in the Ministry of Community Development, Mother and Child Health. 'Following this decision to open consultations, the NGOs have withdrawn the court injunction/petition against Government to allow for the fruitful deliberations and the process of reviewing the law,' Mr. Chipenzi said. He said a consultant would soon be engaged to commence the revision of the Act, with a roadmap agreed upon to have the law enacted by July 2015. 'We agreed that we should come up with a law that would be fair for both parties as we try to promote transparency and accountability in the operations of the NGOs,' he said. He commended government for heeding the calls for consultation on the NGO Act as Civil Society Organisations and the NGOs were partners in development complimenting each other's works. This was the beginning of the review process of the NGO Act No. 16 of 2009. He was optimistic that the spirit that government had exhibited to engage in consultation with civil society over the NGO Act review process should be extended to the Constitution making process.

Government reiterated its commitment to reviewing the NGO Act as stated in the PF manifesto[10] that the NGO Act would be amended within 90 days and the issue was scheduled to have been tabled before Cabinet in that year (2011) and then consultations with stakeholders, including the Council of NGOs, on the review of the NGO Act also undertaken and concluded. Despite joint roadmap on the review being developed and agreed on, the review process procrastinated to date.

This directive from government to NGOs triggered a court process which was led by seven (7) NGOs which petitioned the government to stop the threats but instead repeal the law that restricted Civil Society work and align the law with International Standards.[11] The decision the government wanted to take could have violated the fundamental right to association. The HRW (2023) raised the concern regarding government's treatment of CSOs and urged the government of Zambia to 'take decisive and immediate action to repeal a law that unduly restricts the activities of nongovernmental organisations and civil society groups that operate in the country'. After a long deliberation, the government agreed to settle the matter outside court and agreed to embark on the repeal and replacement of the NGO Act and retreated its threats on deregistration. Since then, the NGOs have been free to register with any registration authority of their choice. However, the Zambian Ministry of Community

[10] PF Manifesto, 2011.
[11] Human Rights Watch, 2023.

Development and Social Services announced in mid-2023 that the process of repealing and replacing the NGO Act number 16 of 2009 was near completion. Minister in Charge, Doreen Mwamba, was confident that the bill would be enacted into law due to the work that has already been put in place. 'We have made significant progress in the process of repealing and replacing the NGO Act number 16 of 2009. The new law will create a road map for registering all NGOs and establish a firm legal framework that will regulate the sector,' said Minister Mwamba as quoted in Lusaka Times Online of 28 February 2023.

The argument is on the premise that once the new bill is enacted, it will provide a more conducive operational environment for the growth and development of NGOs in Zambia, and Ms. Mwamba urged all NGOs to fully participate in the process and acquire knowledge in the terrorist financing outreach and awareness meetings scheduled to take place throughout the year. 'We need to work together to ensure that the NGO sector in Zambia is well regulated and that it operates within the confines of the law. We are undertaking a comprehensive NGO terrorist financing risk assessment to protect the sector,' added Minister Mwamba while appreciating the work of the NGOs during the World NGO Day celebrations themed 'Celebrating Non-governmental Organization localised as celebrating the works of Non-governmental Organizations in Zambia'. 'The commemoration is an opportunity for the government to appreciate the work of NGOs. The new law will provide a legal framework that is better suited to the needs of NGOs in Zambia, ultimately promoting democracy and the protection of human rights,' said Minister Mwamba.

To demonstrated this intolerant towards CSOs then Foundation for Democratic Process (FODEP) Executive Director, McDonald Chipenzi and Others v. The People case in the High Court of Zambia highlighted the heightened shrinking civic space in the country. This is a case in which Chipenzi and others were arrested under Section 67 of the Penal Code and tried and acquitted later.[12] The High Court of Zambia found that Section 67 of Zambia's Penal Code, prohibiting the publication of false information likely to cause public fear, violated the Constitution as it did not amount to a reasonable justification for limiting the freedom of expression. The facts were that on 10 December 2013, the McDonald Chipenzi and two others (applicants) published an article in the *Daily Nation Newspaper Limited*, alleging that Zambia Police Service was secretly

[12] Global Freedom of Expression, 2014.

recruiting new police officers against the dictates of the Constitution and that it had recruited a number of foreign militia into the main stream of police service. The government subsequently arrested the applicants and charged them with the violation of Section 67 of the Penal Code. The law imposes maximum of three years imprisonment for dissemination of false information 'likely to cause fear and alarm to the public or to disturb the public peace'. The Applicants challenged the constitutionality of Section 67, arguing that the law was inconsistent with Article 20 of Zambia's Constitution, which guarantees '[The] freedom to impart and communicate ideas and information without interference'. On the other hand, the government contended that the criminal prosecution conformed to Article 20(3) of the Constitution as a reasonable measure required for the purpose of protecting the reputations, rights and freedoms of others.

Late High Court Justice Isaac Chali delivered the opinion of the Court on 14 December 2014, exactly a year after the arrest of the applicants. The main issue was whether Section 67 of Zambia's Penal Code was a reasonable justification in limiting the freedom of expression by imposing criminal sanctions for publishing false information likely to cause public fear. The Court first analysed the scope of the law. It held that Section 67 was impermissibly overbroad as it was capable of not only prohibiting false news but also those with honest beliefs as to the truthfulness of their statements. According to the Court, the law virtually restricts '*any statement which does not meet the majority definition of truth and lends force to the argument that the law could be used or abused in circular fashion essentially to permit the prosecution of news which is unpopular in the ears of those in authority*'. Furthermore, the Court ruled that the law violated the Constitution because it allowed the government to shift the burden of proving the elements of the crime, as it required the accused to prove the lack of knowledge of the falsity of his or her statement. Also, the Court rejected the notion that the law was reasonably related to the protection of public order because the liability for prosecution and conviction was not dependent upon any actual or imminent occurrence of public fear or disturbance. According to the Court, the law was merely intended to prevent remote and uncertain dangers arising out of dissemination of false news. For forgoing reasons, the Court invalidated Section 67 of Zambia's Penal Code for being inconsistent with the constitutional protection of freedom of expression. The prosecution promised to appeal the decision of the court but did not. Number of other individuals faced the same charge before various courts and police stations. With this judgement, these charges were dropped. However, in countering this development, the government hastily enacted the Cyber Security and Cyber Crimes law in 2021, which also contained a similar section as was section 67. A number of individuals were arrested using this law.

Another example of restricted civic space was recorded in September 2017 when Police in the capital city—Lusaka—arrested six (6) civil society practitioners who marched to Parliament to demonstrate against the purchase of 42 fire tenders at the exorbitant cost of US$42 million. Those arrested were Alliance for Community Action (ACA) Executive Director Laura Miti, Patriots for Economic Progress (PeP) president Sean Tembo, singer and political activist Chama Fumba aka. *Pilato*, Zambia Council for Social Development Executive Director Lewis Mwape and several other protesters. Police Spokesperson, then Esther Mwata Katongo, confirmed the arrest and charge of 'disobeying lawful orders' contrary to clause 127 Cap 87 of the laws of Zambia against the six with the offence of 'disobeying lawful orders' contrary to clause 127 Cap 87 of the laws of Zambia. Laura Miti, singer Pilato and three other demonstrators were released around 23 hours from police custody in various police cells such as Garden, Emmasdale, among others, and were released on paying K2000 police bond each pending court appearance on 27 October 2017. The six were forcibly arrested after they staged a demonstration outside Parliament buildings over the controversial purchase of 42 fire trucks at a cost of US$42 million.[13] One of the accused, Sean Tembo, retorted, 'This is to advise that we have been released from the unlawful detention by the Zambia Police Service following our lawful protest at Parliament this afternoon over the $42 million fire tender scandal. I will issue a comprehensive press statement tomorrow morning.' 'This is to advise that we have been released from the unlawful detention by the Zambia Police Service following our lawful protest at Parliament this afternoon over the $42 million fire tender scandal. I will issue a comprehensive press statement tomorrow morning.'

Another clear act of intimidation and threats from the government then on CSO operations and space was during the campaign for a people-driven constitution in the period 2011-2015. This when the PF Secretary-General and Minister of Justice then, Wynter Kabimba, threatens Youths holding dialogues and other stakeholders over the Constitution making process with arrests on 16 December 2012. In his letter entitled 'Parallel

[13] *Lusaka Times*, 2017.

Workshops on the Constitution Making Process' reminded the organisation concerned never to conduct parallel dialogue workshops that were not under the auspice of a body constituted to draft the Constitution of Zambia or else face the wrath of the police. By copy of his letter, the Zambia Police Service Inspector General was informed to take stern action against any leader of the organisation that would organise such a workshop.

Musician Chama Fumba aka Pilato was in 2018 forced to leave the country, according to him, 'in order to stay alive'. Extracting from his Facebook post posted on 25 January 2018, the controversial musician Pilato spoke out for the first time since fleeing Zambia amidst threats on his life. Writing from a secret location, Pilato said he was forced to leave Zambia and stay in the bush for 25 days after PF cadres threatened his life. He explained that he has been warned that he will be snatched even from the courts of law or that even if he dared to go to hide in the American Embassy, he would still be snatched and dealt with. Pilato observed that Zambia had a President who became rich just by being alive and that in his attempt to share this story, he was threatened with death. 'Today I am writing from a foreign country not because I chose to but because I chose life. The 14th of January 2018 was my daughter's birthday, on this day I usually take her and the sister out for a Pizza but this time I couldn't. I called and spoke to her and she asked when I was going back home, I cut the call because I didn't know when. I have stopped calling home now because I don't know what to say to them,' he wrote. Amnesty International issued an alert over Pilato, who went into exile in an undisclosed country fearing for his life.

Below is the full statement issued by Pilato;

AWAY FROM ZAMBIA

It doesn't matter where you claim to be going, you will only go where you are heading. If one is on the bus to Chawama, even if they claim to be going to Woodlands, they will only go as far as the bus can go. So it doesn't matter what we claim to be, we are what we act. The greatest act of belief is not in the claiming but in the acting.

Do we live what we believe?

Zambia is a beautiful country with very beautiful and peaceful people. It is sad that those that we've given our power to manage and rule our land are taking advantage of this fact. Today I am writing from a foreign country not because i chose to but because i chose life.

It is important to die for a cause but it is even more important to live for it. My country Zambia is blessed with resources, copper, water, youths and so many other great things. If these resources are not benefiting the people of Zambia now, what will they benefit from in the future when we will not have any more copper? If our resources don't improve the living standards of our people now what will?

I am an artist who lives among the poor people, these poor people speak to me daily. It is in their eyes i look every day and i always pray that they don't lose hope. I pray that they keep believing for a better future. I pray that they still look at the national flag and be proud that they belong to a country that is not anything lesser than other countries. I pray that every Zambian will walk tall among his or her other human beings from other countries.

I pray for dignity for my people. But what is dignity without a proper healthcare? When our people can't find drugs in hospitals? What is their dignity when students are brutally beaten by the state police for asking for meal allowances from their own government? When majority of our young people can't find jobs and when they do it's under very inhumane conditions, what is their dignity?

When our people cry for proper health care, our leaders use that to enrich themselves. They use our cries to steal. They buy ambulances at prices that not even rich country can consider buying. When our youths cry for jobs, they sign a $1.2 billion road construction contracts and say our people will have jobs. A road that costs less in other places. We have a president who became rich just by being alive. In my attempt to share this story, I was threatened with death. I was forced to leave home and stayed in the bush for 25 days for merely sharing this truth.

The 14th of January 2018 was my daughter's birthday, on this day i usually take her and the sister out for a Pizza but this time i couldn't. I called and spoke to her and she asked when I was going back home, i cut the call because i didn't know when. I have stopped calling home now because I don't know what to say to them.

In my lonely moments I ask myself, is it worth fighting for the good of my people even when it means endangering my own life? Why can't I be like many other artists that just sing and make money? A bigger part of me reminds me that I am a part of every human being that has shared their pain and sorrows with me. I want to be alive and safe but I only deserve the life that i can fight and speak for. I want my children to go to school, but they only deserve the education that every child in my country can get. I want proper health-care for Christina and Abishai but only that which every child in Zambia can get. This is why my life is threatened. This is why I am where i am today.

I have been warned that i will be snatched even from the courts of law. I have been warned that even if I dared to go hide in the American Embassy I would still be snatched and dealt with. I don't want to die for this fight, I want to live for it.

> *The police officers have lost power to political blood thirsty Satanists who are beating and killing people with impunity. These demons attacked people at the graveyard and no one has accounted for that. I refuse to die or be beaten by such evil imitations of humanity. I will live to see the greatness of my people....and of my country*
>
> *To my family and friends, I am well and safe, please whenever you can check on my family.*
>
> *Thank you.*

On 20 October 2018, News Informants Zambia reported another incident attacking the operations of the civil society where Police Arrest Men of God at Ndola Baptist Church. The disruption by the police was triggered by informants who alerted the police that a meeting of pastors had in the midst opposition official, Brian Mwiinga. The pastors and the NGO officials—Centre for Trade Policy and Development (CTPD) that organised the meeting—were arrested and charged for 'unlawful assembly'. Pastor George Palo together with others were arrested from Ndola Central Baptist Church after the pastors from different churches on the Copperbelt convened to talk about the proposed 2019 National Budget. But before they went far with the meeting police arrived at the church and arrested six (6) senior men of God. When the pastors asked the police why they disrupted the meeting and who sent them to come to the place of worship, the police removed the teargas canisters and threatened to throw them in the church if they were not dispersing. Among those arrested are CTPD Head of Programmes and Research, Brian Mwiinga and his counterpart, Isiah Mbewe, Head of Communications.

How the Zambian CSOs Navigated Brutal Rein

A number of strategies were employed among the conformity by adopting the phrase 'if you can't beat them join them' and those who refused to conform were the most harassed, discriminated and marginalised. A number of CSOs started assuming the 'praise singing' postures for the ruling party in order to make peace with the ruling elites. Others abandoned advocacy work altogether and joined service-related organisations which were more user-friendly by the regime than human rights and advocacy CSOs. Since local donors were also polluted with the ruling regime's propaganda against those CSOs as 'agents of regime change' and puppets of 'foreign', especially Western countries, many CSOs depended on overseas developmental agencies for support and survival. Some fled the country to save their lives while others used social media to communicate their dissatisfaction with still others using the bush as spaces for airing their grievances. In terms of exercising their rights to assembly, association and expression, some CSOs sought the interpretation of the court as to the constitutionality of the actions of the state, e.g. the McDonald Chipenzi and Others v. The People and Laura Miti and 5 Others v. The People cases. In Other words, few CSOs survived the onslaught from the regime. To navigate the restrictive laws of freedom of assembly, the country saw the use of social media platforms as places of assembly such as WhatsApp and Facebook while others exploited the provisions in the Public Order Act that exempted certain churches from seeking permission for their assemblies. These religious spaces/platforms were used to assemble and air their concerns of the governance of the country though these churches were not spared from intimidation and harassment leading to some denying CSOs from using their spaces. Just like in the use of media platforms such as TV and radio stations where a number of radio and TV stations denied perceived anti-ruling party CSO leaders from featuring on their platforms with those who insisted facing closure or suspension of their operating licences, the churches too followed suit in denying the CSOs for fear of such actions from the state and party leadership.

Youth Growing Awareness of Government Debt to the Outside World

There is no reliable data found indicating the youth's growing awareness of government debt to the outside world and also domestically. However, general debates are raging on traditional and social media platforms regarding the negative effects of debt economic, social growth and political stability of the country. As the country was heading towards the General Election in 2021, Zambia's debt stock had reached its peak of unsustainability. Many citizens and civil society were concerned with the debt stock the country was under and described the country as under debt stress. For example, in 2021, Zambia's overall debt burden reached 123% of the country's GDP according to the International Monetary Fund. As at end June 2021, Zambia's total public debt was US$ equivalent to 26.44bn excluding interest arrears, and US$ equivalent to 26.96bn including interest arrears. At the end of June 2021, external stock, excluding interest arrears, of Central Government Debt guaranteed state-owned enterprises (SOEs) loans and non-guaranteed SOEs loans, amounted to US$12.91bn, US$1.57bn and US$195.7 mn, respectively. This included Central Government, guaranteed and non-guaranteed state-owned enterprises liabilities, denominated in both foreign and local currencies.[14] This is the debt stock which the Hichilema's government inherited in 2021. For instance, the domestic debt alone was estimated at K78 billion in August 2021 and is now currently believed to stand at K235 billion. However, as at September 2021, according to Minister of Finance Dr. Situmbeko Musokotwane, the audited Central Government Domestic Debt was K46.9billion with fuel arrears standing at $477.79. 'The stock of audited Central Government Domestic Arrears, or Pending Bills, excluding fuel and electricity, amounted to K46.9 billion as at end June 2021 from K41.0 billion in December 2020. The bulk of the arrears were to road contractors, suppliers of goods and services, Value Added Tax (VAT) refunds and personnel related emoluments to Public Service Workers.'[15] The National Democratic Institute for International Affairs (NDI) report revealed that Zambia, in November 2020, made headlines when it became the first African nation to default on its debt repayment to foreign lenders during the COVID-19 global health crisis that beset the country.

While many African nations made significant progress in reducing their debt burdens in the 1990s and 2000s, Zambia steadily took on more and more loans to finance large infrastructure projects and government spending during the PF regime to the extent that by 2021, Zambia's overall debt burden reached 123% of the country's GDP. Such heavy Public Debt Burdens posed a threat to long-term economic stability and impact negatively on service delivery for citizens, especially to the youth, particularly, during emergency contexts such as the COVID-19 pandemic. This is because government would have to dedicate larger percentages of its budget to debt repayment. It goes without an argument that Zambia's spiralling debt became a salient issue in the 2021 General Election to which the incumbent government promised, in its campaign messages, to finalise

[14] GRZ (2021) Summary of the Republic of Zambia's Public Sector Debt—As at End—June 2021.

[15] National Assembly of Zambia; Budget Address by Honourable Dr. Situmbeko Musokotwane, MP, Minister of Finance and National Planning Delivered to the National Assembly On Friday, 29th October 2021.

and clinch an International Monetary Fund (IMF) and World Bank bailout package after the elections which has been done. Debt and other economic and social issues proved to be a powerful motivation for the almost 60% (mainly youth and rural people) of Zambians to vote for a new political leadership that promised a different approach to the economic malaise the country was subjected to.

After the elections, social and economic pressure, however, continued to mount on the new administration to follow through on its campaign promises to prioritise transparency and accountability in legal reforms around debt contraction.[16] In response to Zambia's growing debt burden and increasing calls from citizens for action, the Civil Society Organisation called Debt Alliance, a collection of 42 Zambian civil society organisations from a variety of sectors that sought/seeks to improve public debt management by advocating for increased transparency and accountability in government borrowing and greater parliamentary oversight of loan contraction, was launched in November 2020. The view of this civil society alliance on debt formed at the closing part of the PF government was that the debt was unsustainable and the growing awareness of government debt to the outside world, i.e. what the Hichilema government came to inherit, was injuring economic growth and affected job creation among the youth, education delivery and healthcare, among others. The CSO Debt Alliance took a broad approach to its advocacy efforts, tackling the debt problem from multiple angles, including through legal analysis by conducting a legislative review of the existing Loans, Grants, and Guarantees Authorisation (LGGA) Act, which guides the Zambian government's process of managing its debt, and identified gaps and weaknesses in the legal framework. The Alliance drafted and presented a model Debt Management Bill to the government.

Zambia had to resort to Debt Restructuring Process, which has been ably highlighted by ACA's Maila Pride, Citizen Journalist. Maila's summary of the process argues that the debt burden for Zambia, which according to Reuters News Agency, involved negotiating with creditors to reduce interest rates, extend repayment terms, or decrease loan balances with the aim to make debt more manageable by lowering monthly payments, reducing interest rates or cutting the total amount owed. Fortunately, in March 2024, the Government of the Republic of Zambia and the Steering

[16] Lavu Phiri, Resident Programme Manager, Zambia; Coretta Mwanza, Senior Programme Assistant, Zambia; Kerianne DiBattista (2022).

Committee of the Ad Hoc Creditor Committee reached an agreement in principle on the key commercial terms of a proposed restructuring transaction for the country's Eurobonds maturing in 2022, 2024 and 2027. Below is the background to Zambia's Debt Restructuring Process which Maila tries to explain by stating that emergence of the Debt Challenges popped up between 2019 and 2020. During this period, the country faced difficulties repaying international bonds ('Eurobonds') and other debts. In May 2020, the Zambian government, under President Edgar Lungu, hired French firm Lazard to advise on restructuring foreign debts, which were then officially estimated at \$11 billion. Zambia requested debt payment freezes under the G20 Debt Service Suspension Initiative (DSSI) in June 2020 and defaulted on a \$42.5 million Eurobond payment in November 2020, becoming Africa's first pandemic-era sovereign defaulter in 2021. With the 2021 General Election past us and a new Transition of Leadership is put in the place, in August 2021, President Hakainde Hichilema's government took office. The new Finance Minister revealed that Zambia's external debt had risen to \$17 billion, with debts to Chinese lenders nearly double the previous official figures. Between 2022 and 2023, the Official Creditors took action and in June 2022, an Official Creditor Committee (OCC) was formed to address Zambia's debt, co-chaired by China and France. In July 2022, the OCC committed to providing debt relief, paving the way for a \$1.3 billion International Monetary Fund (IMF) rescue package. By June 2023, the OCC agreed to restructure \$6.3 billion of Zambia's loans. In late 2023, government faced the challenges with bondholders. Zambia's government reached a preliminary agreement with bondholders in October 2023 to consolidate \$3 billion in Eurobonds into two instruments with extended payment terms. However, in November 2023, the OCC vetoed a revised deal with bondholders, citing insufficient debt relief. This caused bondholders to withdraw from negotiations, stalling progress.

In 2024, there were renewed efforts to try and bear fruit from such processes such that in January 2024, Zambian officials travelled to negotiate with Chinese creditors, leading to restructuring of the agreements with India and China in February 2024. In March 2024, Zambia reached a deal-in-principle with private bondholders, marking a significant step towards resolving its debt crisis. Therefore, the current Status of Debt Restructuring is that the 2024 Agreement addresses Zambia's Eurobonds, namely \$750 million (due in 2022); \$1 billion (due in 2024); \$1.25 billion (due in 2027), and includes key aspects of the Agreement such as bondholders foregoing $840 million in claims; $2.5 billion in cash flow relief through Reduced Debt Servicing Payments (RDSP) during the IMF programme period and the new terms to attract investments, create jobs for the youth and fund urgent priorities like disaster responses.

With the foregoing, the impact of debt restructuring on citizens cannot be overemphasised. The effects include, but not limited to, Reduced Debt Servicing Costs; Zambia's External Debt Repayments have historically consumed a large portion of the national budget, leaving limited resources for critical sectors, e.g. in 2022, K51.3 billion was spent on External Debt Servicing and in 2023, K13.3 billion allocated to debt repayments. Under the new agreement, funds previously used for External Debt Servicing can now be redirected towards Education Sector [job recruitment of teachers and improvement of facilities]; Healthcare Sector [procurement of medicine and recruitment of nurses]; Infrastructure Sector [road construction and maintenance]; Energy Sector [Importation of electricity]; Local Development Sector [Increased Constituency Development Fund (CDF) allocations and Potential for Economic Growth].

The restructuring agreement almost done, the expectation stabilised the economy by creating an enabling environment for investments and growth, generating jobs, and reducing the cost of living. However, the challenges persist such as despite the positive strides, the cost of living remains high. According to the Jesuit Centre for Theological Reflection (JCTR), the Basic Needs and Nutrition Basket for a family of five in Lusaka rose to K10, 701.13 in May 2024, a K352.87 increase compared to April 2024.[17] In this regard, Zambia's debt restructuring agreement is a critical step towards economic recovery. By easing the financial burden of External Debt Servicing, the government has the potential to channel resources into essential services that directly benefit citizens. However, the success of this process will be judged by its tangible impact on everyday life, including job creation for the youth, improved public services to citizens and a reduced cost of living for all. Citizens remain optimistic yet vigilant, expecting the government to ensure that the benefits of debt restructuring translate into meaningful improvements in their standard of living.[18]

[17] Alliance for Community Action (ACA), 2024.

[18] Ibid.

Conclusion

The above citations and many not cited in this chapter were the actual operating environment for civil society during the PF era. In addition, legal impediments through the use of existing laws and development of new restrictive laws on the citizens, the civic space was suffocated at an accelerated rate in the 10 years of the PF rule. Therefore, Zambia's human civic, media and political spaces during this era deteriorated remarkably and speedily. Ordinary people, civil society organisations and opposition political party supporters and leaders were increasingly subjected to a restrictive operating CSOs environment. A number of CSOs were unable to freely assemble publicly, protest, demonstrate or engage in public demonstrations or protest against government actions including wearing party regalia of the opposing political alignment without being subjected to intimidation, harassment by the ruling party supporters popularly called cadres and the police. Therefore, 'if you don't like something, change it. If you can't change it, change your attitude,' was the order of the day.

Sources

Action Aid Zambia (AAZ) (2019), Time for Action: *Shrinking space in Zambia*, Policy Brief, 21 March 2019; Shrinking space in Zambia | ActionAid International;

Alliance for Community Action (ACA), (2024), Speak Up Youth Fact Sharing: Zambia's Debt Restructuring Process, 20 June, 2024

Amnesty International Report (2021), Zambia: Ruling by fear and repression, June 28, 2021 Index Number: AFR 63/4057/2021; Zambia: Ruling by fear and repression - Amnesty International;

Global Freedom of Expression (2014), McDonald Chipenzi & Others v. The People, (HPR/03/2014) [2014], https://globalfreedomofexpression.columbia.edu/cases/chipenzi-v-the-people/;

GRZ (2021), Ministry of Finance and National Planning; Summary of the Republic of Zambia's Public Sector Debt - As at End-June 2021, GRZ. https://www.lusakatimes.com/wp-content/uploads/2021/10/End-June-2021-Public-Debt-Summary.pdf

Human Rights Watch (HRW), 2023, 29 March, 2023; Zambia: Repeal Law That Restricts Civil Society: Align Domestic Laws with International Standards; https://www.hrw.org/news/2023/03/29/zambia-repeal-law-restricts-civil-society.

Lusaka Times (2012), 6 December, 2012, "Justice Minister Wynter Kabimba threatens Youths holding dialogues over the Constitution making process with Arrests." https://www.lusakatimes.com/2012/12/16/justice-minister-wynter-kabimba-threatens-youths-holding-dialogues-constitution-making-process-arrests/

Lusaka Voice (2014), Government to undertake a review of the NGO Act of 2009 https://lusakavoice.com/2014/02/28/government-to-undertake-a-review-of-the-ngo-act-of-2009/;

Phiri, L., Mwanza, C., & Dibattista, K., (2022), Tackling Zambia's Debt Problem: Supporting Debt Management Reforms through CSO Collaboration. NDI publication, https://www.ndi.org/our-stories/tackling-zambia-s-debt-problem-supporting-debt-management-reforms-through-cso#:~:text=In%202021%2C%20Zambia%E2%80%99s%20overall%20debt%20burden%20reached%20123%25,country%E2%80%99s%20GDP%20according%20to%20the%20International%20Monetary%20Fund.

New Diggers Newspapers, "Police arrest Laura, others" 29 September 2017; Police arrest Laura, others – Zambia: News Diggers!

PRMC (2017), PRMC Policy Analysis of The Non-Governmental Organisations' Act No. 16 Of 2009: "Need To Regulate But Not Curtail Non-Governmental Organisations' Unique Role To Supplement Government Service"; https://www.pmrczambia.com/wp-content/uploads/2017/08/Policy-Analysis_NGO-Act_2009-f.pdf;

Irene Khan, the Special Rapporteur on Freedom of Expression, Preliminary Observations by Irene Khan, Special Rapporteur on Freedom of Opinion and Expression, at the end of her visit to Zambia (20–31 January 2025). 2025-01-31-sr-feedex-eom-visit-zambia-en.pdf

Irene Khan, the Special Rapporteur on Freedom of Expression, Press Release, 29 August 2024. Zambia must immediately halt downward spiral of infringements on fundamental freedoms: UN experts. Zambia must immediately halt downward spiral of infringements on fundamental freedoms: UN experts | OHCHR

Lusaka Times Online Media, 13 September, 2013, "Government threatens NGOs with deregistration if they don't register under NGO Act", Zambia: Government threatens NGOs with deregistration if they don't register under NGO Act

Lusaka Times Online Newspaper, "Laura Miti, Pilato and others released", September 30, 2017. Zambia : Laura Miti, Pilato and others released

Sfeir-Younis, A. (2004), "The Role of Civil Society in Foreign Policy: A New Conceptual Framework". Seton Hall Journal of Diplomacy and international Relations, p. 29–32.

Zambia Eye Online media, 3 June, 2014, "Good luck, remove NGOs from Zambia, FODEP dares Govt", Good luck, remove NGOs from Zambia, FODEP dares Govt - Zambian Eye

Correction to: The Economic Transformation and Political Economy of Zambia

Correction to:

S. Chan, *The Economic Transformation and Political Economy of Zambia*, Palgrave Studies in African and Development Economics, https://doi.org/10.1007/978-3-031-93030-0

This book was inadvertently published without the following contributing authors' names: Hangwei Li, Cynthia M. Kamwengo, and McDonald Chipenzi. These contributing authors' names have now been updated in the revised versions.

The updated versions of these chapters can be found at
https://doi.org/10.1007/978-3-031-93030-0_8
https://doi.org/10.1007/978-3-031-93030-0_9
https://doi.org/10.1007/978-3-031-93030-0_10

S. Chan, *The Economic Transformation and Political Economy of Zambia*, Palgrave Studies in African and Development Economics,
https://doi.org/10.1007/978-3-031-93030-0_11

Bibliography

Aarnes, Dag and Mike Taylor, 'Confidence, Investment and Growth: Economic Developments and the 2001 Elections in Zambia', *African Social Research*, 45/46, 2000/2001, pp 151–196.

Action Aid Zambia (AAZ) (2019), Time for Action: Shrinking space in Zambia, Policy Brief, 21 March 2019. https://actionaid.org/publications/2019/shrinking-space-zambia

Africa Confidential. "Bonds, Bills and Ever Bigger Debts." Africa Confidential 59, no. 18. (2018). https://www.africa-confidential.com/article-preview/id/12424/Bonds%2c_bills_and_ever_bigger_debts

Amnesty International Report (2021), 'Zambia: Ruling by fear and repression.' June 28, 2021 Index Number: AFR 63/4057/2021; https://www.amnesty.org/en/documents/afr63/4057/2021/en/

Anglin, Douglas G. *Zambian Crisis Behaviour: Confronting Rhodesia's Unilateral Declaration of Independence, 1965-1966*, Montreal & Kingston: McGill-Queen's University Press, 1994.

Brautigam, Deborah, & Xiaoyang, Tang. (2011). African Shenzhen: China's special economic zones in Africa. *The Journal of Modern African Studies*, 49(1), 27–54.

Brown, Robin. *The Secret Society: Cecil John Rhodes's Plans for a New World Order*, London: Penguin, 2015.

Burns, John F. 'Rhodesians Strike at Zambian Capital in bid to get Nkomo.' *New York Times*, 14 April 1979, https://www.nytimes.com/1979/04/14/

S. Chan, *The Economic Transformation and Political Economy of Zambia*, Palgrave Studies in African and Development Economics, https://doi.org/10.1007/978-3-031-93030-0

archives/rhodesians-strike-at-zambian-capital-in-bid-to-get-nkomo-rebels-in.html

Carrington, Peter. *Reflect on Things Past*, London: Collins, 1988.

Cerutti, Paolo Omar, Davison Gumbo, Kaala Moombe, George Schoneveld, Robert Nasi, Nils Bourland, & Xiaoxue Weng. (2022). Informality, global capital, rural development and the environment: Mukula (rosewood) trade between China and Zambia.

Chan, Stephen. *Exporting Apartheid: Foreign Policies in Southern Africa 1978-1988*, N.Y.: St. Martins, 1990.

——— *Kaunda and Southern Africa: Image and Reality in Foreign Policy*, London: I.B. Tauris, 1992.

——— 'The Memory of Violence: trauma in the writings of Alexander Kanengoni and Yvonne Vera and the idea of unreconciled citizenship in Zimbabwe', *Third World Quarterly*, 26:2, 2005, pp. 369–382.

——— 'China's Foreign Policy and Africa: The Rise and Fall of China's Three World's Theory', *The Round Table*, 296, 1985a, p 378.

——— *The Commonwealth Observer Group in Zimbabwe: A Personal Memoir*, Gweru: Mambo Press, 1985b.

——— *The Morality of China in Africa: The Middle Kingdom and the Dark Continent*, London: Zed, 2013.

Chanda, Donald (ed.), Democracy in Zambia: Key Speeches of President Chiluba 1991/2, Lusaka: *Africa Press Trust*, 1992.

Cheeseman, Nic and Marja Hinfelaar, 'Parties, platforms, and political mobilization: The Zambian presidential election of 2008', *African Affairs*, 109:434, pp 51–76.

Cheyeka, Austin M. 'Zambia, a 'Christian nation' in Post Movement for Multiparty Democracy (MMD) Era, 2011-2016', *International Journal of Humanities and Social Sciences*, 6:7, 2016, pp. 159–172.

Chipimo, Elias C. Jr. *Unequal to the Task?*, Lusaka: self-published, 2010.

Chisalu, Philip, and Ulande Nkomesha. "It's Difficult for China to Cut Zambia's Debt Because It Has Its Own Challenges – IMF." *News Diggers*, 25 January 2023.

Clarke, Roy and Trevor Ford, *The Worst of Kalaki and the Best of Yuss*, Lusaka: Bookworld, 2004.

Davidow, Jeffrey. *A Peace in Southern Africa – The Lancaster House Conference on Rhodesia*, 1979, Boulder: Westview, 1984.

Dynamic, Beyongo. (2016). Fighting the race to the bottom: Regulating Chinese investment in Zambian mines. *Made in China Journal*. Available at: https://madeinchinajournal.com/2016/09/27/fighting-the-race-to-the-bottom-regulating-chinese-investment-in-zambian-mines/

Ferguson, James. *Expectations of Modernity: Myths and Meaning on the Zambian Copperbelt*, Berkeley: University of California Press, 1999.

Fraser, Alastair. 'Post-populism in Zambia: Michael Sata's rise, demise and legacy', *International Political Science Review*, 38:4, 2017, pp. 456–472.

Fraser, Alastair & Miles Larmer (eds.), *Zambia, Mining and Neoliberalism: Boom and Bust on the Globalized Copperbelt*, N.Y.: Palgrave Macmillan, 2010.

Gifford, Paul. *African Christianity: Its Public Role*, London: Hurst, 1998.

Goodfellow, T., & Huang, Z. (2021). Contingent infrastructure and the dilution of 'Chineseness'. *Environment and Planning: Economy and Space, 53*(4), 655–674.

Gulhati, Ravi. *Impasse in Zambia: The Economics and Politics of Reform*, Washington DC: World Bank, 1989.

Hall, Richard. The High Price of Principles: Kaunda and the White South, London: Hodder & Stoughton, 1969.

Hampwaye, G., Carmody, P., & Ramaloko, P. M. (2023). China-Zambia engagements: Is there change, what has changed, and why? *Journal of Contemporary East Asia Studies*, 12(1), 179–198.

Hatch, John. *Two African Statesmen: Kaunda of Zambia and Nyerere of Tanzania*, London: Secker & Warburg, 1976.

Henriot, Peter. "Retreat of the State: Political Consequences and Social Implications for Zambia." In *Development Review* 1997, edited by Trocaire, 39–60. Dublin: Trocaire, 1997.

Human Rights Watch (HRW), 2023, 29 March, 2023; Zambia: Repeal Law That Restricts Civil Society: Align Domestic Laws with International Standards; https://www.hrw.org/news/2023/03/29/zambia-repeal-law-restricts-civil-society.

Iliffe, John. The African Poor: a history, Cambridge: Cambridge University Press, 1987.

Kamwengo, Cynthia M. "Social Media Debates on Zambia's Evolving Relations with the West and East: Trends and Implications." *Megatrends Policy Brief*, 2024.

Kaunda, Kenneth. *Zambia Shall be Free*. London: Heinemann, 1962.

——— *A Humanist in Africa*, London: Longman Green, 1966

Kirsch, Thomas G. *Spirits and Letters: Writing and Charisma in African Christianity*, N.Y.: Berghahn, 2008.

Kopiński, D., Carmody, P., & Taylor, I. (2023). *The political economy of Chinese FDI and spillover effects in Africa*. Springer Nature.

Larmer, Miles. *Rethinking African Politics: A History of Opposition on Zambia*. London: Routledge, 2016.

Larmer, Miles and Alastair Fraser, 'Of Cabbages and King Cobra: Populist politics and Zambia's 2006 election', *African Affairs*, 106:425, 2007, pp. 611–638

——— 'At the Crossroads: Mining and Political Change on the Katangese-Zambian Copperbelt', https://www.oxfordhandbooks.com/view/10.1093/

oxfordhb/9780199935369.001.0001/oxfordhb-9780199935369-e-20 2016.

Lee, Ching Kwan. *The Specter of Global China: Politics, Labor and Foreign Investment in Africa*, Chicago: University of Chicago Press, 2017.

Li, H., & Hackenesch, C. (2024). FOCAC 2024: Moving away from large infrastructure deals towards normative power of China. *Megatrends Afrika Spotlight*, 16 September. www.megatrends-afrika.de/en/publication/megatrends-spotlight-38-focac-2024-towards-normative-power-of-china

Libakeni, Yuyi K. *They built Zambia: Zambia's hundred graduates at independence*, Lusaka: Y.K. Libakeni, 2008.

Liu, X. (2024). MoU signed to revitalize TAZARA railway. *Global Times.* Available at: https://www.globaltimes.cn/page/202409/1319255.shtml

Longwe, Sara H. and Roy Clarke, *A gender perspective on the Zambian general election of October 1991*, Lusaka: Zambia Association for Research and Development, 1991.

Lusaka Times Online Newspaper, "Laura Miti, Pilato and others released", September 30, 2017. https://www.lusakatimes.com/2017/09/30/laura-miti-pilato-others-released/

Marten, Lutz and Nancy Kula. 'Zambia: One Zambia, One Nation, Many Languages', in Andrew Simpson (ed.), *Language and National identity in Africa,* Oxford: Oxford University Press, 2008.

Mbozi, Austin. Language Politics in Zambia: Majority Versus Minority Languages, Lusaka: Mulindeti, 2018.

Moorcraft, Paul. *Mugabe's War Machine: Saving or Savaging Zimbabwe?*, Barnsley: Pen & Sword Military, 2011

Pairault, T. (2018). China in Africa: Goods supplier, service provider rather than investor. *Bridges Africa*, 7(5), 17–22.

Phiri, Isabel Apawo. 'President Frederick J.T. Chiluba of Zambia: The Christian Nation and Democracy', *The Journal of Religion in Africa*, 33:4, 2003

Rakner, Lise. *Political and Economic Liberalisation in Zambia 1991-2001.* Uppsala: Nordic Africa Institute, 2003.

Rakner, Lise and Lars Svasand, 'The Quality of Electoral Processes: Zambian Elections 1991-2001', *African Social Research*, 55 & 56, 2003, pp. 1–23.

Ranger, Terence. *Peasant Consciousness and Guerrilla War in Zimbabwe*, London: James Currey, 1985

Ray, R. (2023). 'Small is beautiful': A new era in China's overseas development finance? *Global China Initiative Policy Brief*, 17, 19.

Rukanga, Basillioh. 'Zambian president sacks top judges who ruled in favour of his rival.' *BBC News*, 21 October 2024 https://www.bbc.co.uk/news/articles/cj31k3gkmrko

Saasa, Oliver S. 'Determinants of Zambia's Policies towards the Mining Industry: 1964-1984', in Kwaku Osei-Hwedie and Muna Ndulo (eds.), *Issues in Zambian Development,* Roxbury: Omenana, 1985.

Savage, Rachel and Leigh Thomas. 'Test case Zambia exposes China's rookie status on debt relief—sources.' *Reuters,* 31 May 2022 https://www.reuters.com/world/africa/test-case-zambia-exposes-chinas-rookie-status-debt-relief-sources-2022-05-31/

Scott, Guy. *Adventures in African Politics: A Story in Black & White*, Boulder: Lynne Rienner, 2019.

Serpell, Namwali. 'The Zambian "Afronaut" who wanted to join the Space Race', *The New Yorker*, 11 March 2017.

Setser, Bard & Theo Maret. 'Ten Lessons from Zambia's (incomplete) restructuring', *FT Alphaville—Sovereign Bonds*, 12 September 2023.

Sfeir-Younis, A. (2004), "The Role of Civil Society in Foreign Policy: A New Conceptual Framework". *Seton Hall Journal of Diplomacy and international Relations*, p.29-32.

Shalubala, Chamuka. 'Xi Jinping tells HH he's eager to address Zambia's debt.' *News Diggers,* 31 May 2022 https://diggers.news/local/2022/05/31/xi-jinping-tells-hh-hes-eager-to-address-zambias-debt/

Sishuwa, Sishuwa. 'Zambia: The President's five point plan to stay in power at all costs', *African Arguments*, 1 June 2023, https://africanarguments.org/2023/06/zambia-president-hichilema-five-point-plan-stay-power/

Simutanyi, Neo. 'The Politics of Structural Adjustment in Zambia', *Third World Quarterly,* 17:4, 1996, pp. 825-839.

van Donge, Jan Kees. 'The Plundering of Zambian Resources by Frederick Chiluba and His Friends: A Case Study of the Interaction between National Politics and the International Drive towards Good Governance', *African Affairs*, 108:430, 2009, pp. 69–90.

Zambia Eye Online media, 3 June, 2014, "Good luck, remove NGOs from Zambia, FODEP dares Govt." https://zambianeye.com/good-luck-remove-ngos-from-zambia-fodep-dares-govt/

Index[1]

[1] Note: Page numbers followed by 'n' refer to notes.

S. Chan, *The Economic Transformation and Political Economy of Zambia*, Palgrave Studies in African and Development Economics, https://doi.org/10.1007/978-3-031-93030-0

If you have any concerns about our products,
you can contact us on
ProductSafety@springernature.com

In case Publisher is established outside the EU,
the EU authorized representative is:
Springer Nature Customer Service Center GmbH
Europaplatz 3, 69115 Heidelberg, Germany

Printed by Libri Plureos GmbH
in Hamburg, Germany